TEACHING STRATEGIES OF SOCCER

MICHAEL A. SUTLIFF
EASTERN NEW MEXICO UNIVERSITY

Allyn and Bacon
Boston · London · Toronto · Sydney · Tokyo · Singapore

Series Editor: Suzy Spivey
Series Editorial Assistant: Lisa Davidson
Production Editor: Catherine Hetmansky
Manufacturing Buyer: Aloka Rathnam
Cover Designer: Jenny Burns

ISBN 0-205-15968-0   *TOC*

Printed in the United States of America

10 9 8 7 6 5 4 3 2 1   00 99 98 97 96 95

Dedication

To Cindy, Colin, Brandon, and Taylor who make life worth living.

Acknowledgments

Completion of any project with such magnitude is never possible without the help and support of many. The author would like to thank each individual who made this book possible. First, to my beloved wife, Cindy who read and re-read each page of the manuscript and to my three future soccer players Colin, Brandon, and Taylor who allowed me to write. I would also like to thank photographer Deborah Ward for her willingness and expertise. My sincere appreciation goes to Christopher John "CJ" Burroughs, Melinda Burroughs, and Craig Olgren for agreeing to be photographed. No soccer book is complete without drills, and I would like to thank Scott Hronick, Wandy Graham, and Diane Thomas in Media Services at Eastern New Mexico University for all the hard work. Also, thanks to Dr. Kim Freeland, Chair, Department of Health Human Performance and Recreation at Eastern New Mexico University. Her support and advice on this project was very appreciated. Additionally, a word of thanks to Mari Lynn Dolan. Her efforts in this project were tremendous. I would like to express my thanks to Human Kinetics for allowing me to print each historical drawing. In addition, to the Federation International De Football Association for the authorization to print the official "Laws of the Game." The author would also like to thank the reviewers for all their insight and help. Additionally, I wish to thank my parents, Dale and Nancy Sutliff for their support and suggestions. Finally, the author would like to thank the person who instilled within me a passion for the sport of soccer, Coach Mark Hurlbert.

Preface

The impact that soccer is making on the United States is exciting to witness. Colleges and universities across the country are adding this sport to their curricula. High Schools are making it an interscholastic sport for both men and women. Parents are enthusiastically supporting soccer leagues by enrolling their children into programs. With the increase in participation comes the demand for more teachers. Parents are finding themselves coaching soccer to participants on the youth and junior levels, and often with limited knowledge about the game. This is also true on the High School level. Many teachers are asked to develop and run a soccer program with little or no experience. The colleges and universities are experiencing a similar challenge. Many institutions want to offer soccer as an activity class, but have limited faculty who possess the appropriate expertise. For each of these reasons this book has been written.

Many soccer books are available in this country. Each with a different focus and objective. The objective of this book is to educate the reader in basic and advanced techniques and tactics associated with the game. The reader is lead through a progressive and developmental process of learning soccer techniques, practicing those techniques in various drills, and applying the technique to small then large group situations.

Moving a player towards proficiency in motor skills is a delicate and challenging process. Individuals must first understand or comprehend what the desired tasks involve, be given sufficient time to practice the method without pressure, then placed in challenging situations as their execution becomes proficient. This is how people learn and acquire motor skills, and Teaching Strategies of Soccer has been written in with this concept in mind.

Michael Sutliff

Table of Contents

Chapter Eleven   Systems of Play   198

A Historical Perspective of Soccer

Asia

The origin of soccer, or association football as termed in many parts of the world, is difficult to determine. Facets of the game have been played for thousands of years. Some historians speculate that people have been kicking objects since the beginning of time. Legend has it that cavemen participated in many types of kicking games. Though possible, no evidence exists to substantiate this claim, thus, the true origin of soccer remains a mystery.

According to Van Dalen and Sasajima (1965) evidence does suggest that games resembling soccer were played in China during the Han dynasty (202 B.C. - 8 A.D.). These games were played with a round ball filled with hair and held together by eight pointed strips of leather. The initial purpose of the sport in this country was for military training. The game was called Tsu-Chu, which means Kick-ball. According to one source, participants would pass (kick) the ball in intricate patterns according to specific rules.

汉代宫苑内校阅的足球花赛图

Football during Han Dynasty
Fig. 1.1

The Chinese so enjoyed the game that a general in the Han dynasty disclosed "When they were out in Mongolia, the want of food robbed the army of its morale, but Piao-Chi dug holes in the ground, one of the methods for playing the game, and played football" (Van Dalen & Bennett, 1971). Winners of the game were rewarded with flowers, wine, and even silver while the captain of the losing team was flogged.

The importance of sportsmanship demonstrated throughout the game was very significant. The spirit of good will and personal control is best explained in a poem written by Li Yu (50 - 130 A.D.),

> *"A round ball and a square wall*
> *The ball flying across like the mean*
> *while the teams stand opposed*
> *Captains are appointed and take their places*
> *No allowances are made for relationship*
> *According to unchanging regulations*
> *There must be no partiality*
> *But there must be determination and coolness*
> *Without the slightest irritation at failure*
> *And if all this is necessary for football*
> *How much more for the business of life."*
> *(Giles 1905, p. 16)*

The popularity and love for the game was also evident in the lives of several Chinese Emperors. One particular Emperor who reigned in 1163 A.D. had the playing field covered with an oil cloth and sand to allow the participants to play the game during the rainy seasons. Another emperor so loved the game that he had a minister put to death for criticizing his devotion to the sport. The Chinese also played at night by lighting the field with candles. Participants were advised to keep the body straight as a pencil with hands hanging to their sides. They were instructed to position their feet as if jumping or skipping.

Historians have also discovered evidence of modified soccer games in other parts of Asia. Their findings suggest that in 1004 B.C. the Japanese played a game resembling soccer, using trees as corner markers. Speculation from the works of Li Ju (50 B.C.) suggests the Chinese and Japanese competed against each other in what could be considered the first international match.

Europe

Historians have also looked towards Greece which played a modified soccer game called "episkyres" around 600 B.C. The game closely resembled the Roman sport of "harpastum," which was played in Italy around the same time. The rules of episkyres were quite similar to modern

Football during the Yuan and Ming Dynasty
Fig. 1.2

soccer. According to Marcus (1977), the guidelines required participants to move and play the ball with their feet only; if the ball touched their hands, players would lose possession. A team would score by kicking the ball past a certain section of the goal line.

During the middle ages soccer was a popular but rough sport. Contests in the North and Midlands of England matched entire towns and villages against each other. The objective of the game was to get the ball, by any means, into a goal located at the end of each town. It was not uncommon for players to receive scrapes, cuts, torn clothing, and even broken bones. The violent nature of the game was not respected by the rulers of England. In 1314 King Edward II issued a proclamation banning the game for all citizens, with imprisonment as punishment for breaking the ban. Richard II furthered the ban in 1389, stating it interfered with archery practice.

Three hundred years later the ban was lifted in England, and the popularity of soccer increased. Those who enjoyed the game did so during the entire year, regardless of playing conditions. One favorite winter spot was the frozen River Trent. Those who enjoyed playing on the river's icy surface were confronted with tragedy in 1938 when eight men drowned after the ice collapsed.

Over the next two hundred years the sport witnessed another massive increase in popularity. Leagues were established at universities and schools. The challenge during this time was to delineate a set of rules for consistent play. This was achieved in 1862 when Mr. J.C. Thring, from Uppingham School, developed a code of 10 rules called "The Simplest Game." (Soar & Tyler, 1978).

During the following year a final separation occurred between soccer and rugby, two sports that previously intermixed their rules and regulations. Rugby enthusiasts wanted to maintain the rules of using hands and hacking, the act of kicking the opponents shins, while soccer players did not. These differences lead to the development of the English Football Association in 1863, designed to establish specific rules limiting play to the feet and head.

The growth of soccer spread to other countries, where they established their own Associations. Countries such as Argentina, Scotland, Wales, Germany, and Brazil developed and organized leagues during the late nineteenth and early twentieth century.

Federation Internationale De Football

It became evident that an international organizing body was needed to regulate the sport. In 1904 the first international meeting on soccer was called in Paris, France. The meeting included representatives from Belgium, Denmark, France, Holland, Spain, Sweden, and Switzerland, who formed the Federation Internationale de Football Association (FIFA). This international governing body was designed to arrange and mediate competition between national teams, regulate rules of competition, and solve disputes between national countries and their respected federations.

Football during the Tang Dynasty
Fig. 1.3

During the initial meeting in Paris, the idea to organize a international competition was considered. FIFA met again in 1924 to discuss the options for the first international soccer competition. Finally, in 1930, 24 years after the first meeting in Paris, Uruguay hosted the premier international event for soccer, officially termed the World Cup. While thirteen countries competed in that inaugural event, participation increased to 134 nations taking part in the 1994 tournament, with the United States as the host for the first time.

United States

Soccer has come a long way in the United States since its first introduction during the seventieth century. It is unknown exactly how the sport arrived in America. Some historians propose that British soldiers, even before the Revolutionary War, would play and kick a ball in and around public places in front of amused Americans. Alternate groups suggests soccer was played in Virginia in the early 1600's. Still others find it easy to assume that English colonists who settled in Jamestown brought the sport over from England, along with many other traditional customs.

The origins of soccer in the United States may be in question, but many are confident the sport was popularized with college and public school students, similar to England. The first "official" soccer match was played on November 6, 1869, between two rival colleges, Rutgers and Princeton. Some speculate this was actually the birth of American football, but in reality this match was played under the London Football Association's Laws.

The United States Football Association (USFA) was formed and approved by FIFA in 1913. In 1945, the organization changed its name to the United States Soccer Football Association (USSFA). The present name of the United States Soccer Federation (USSF), in order to clearly delineate itself away from American Football, was finalized in 1974 (Rosenthal, 1981).

The first president of the USSFA was an Englishman named Dr. Ralph Manning. His goal was to make soccer the American past-time during the winter months. To date, this has not occurred. Yet, progress is being made through the efforts of prominent soccer organizations. These include the National Soccer Coaching Association of America (NSCAA), United States Youth Soccer Association (USYSA), and the United States Soccer Federation (USSF). The function of each organization will vary, but universal objectives include: (1) development of programs, (2) conduct coaching clinics for players and coaches, (3) organize conferences, (4) provide leadership and organization, and (5) promote the sport for all age groups in the United States.

The interest in soccer has grown tremendously in the United States, especially on the youth level. Over five million participate between the ages of 6-21. On the college and university level the expansion is also prevalent. Almost 600 teams are fielded a year. Adult soccer is also growing.

Leagues and clubs permeate across the United States. Additionally, the introduction of indoor soccer has allowed players of all age groups to enjoy the sport year round.

Soccer is a very popular participatory and spectator sport for all ages across the United States. With the continued success and interest in soccer, Dr. Manning's dream is becoming a reality.

Teaching Methodologies

Introduction

Teaching soccer is a rewarding experience. When a player improves his/her performance tremendous joy is experienced by the instructor. Possessing the passion for teaching to mastery is invaluable. Yet, many who love the sport of soccer and have enjoyed successful playing experiences, are uncertain about their teaching abilities. Successful instructors are not born. There are specific strategies to learn and techniques to understand before one can become a successful instructor. Outlining these concepts is the focus of this chapter. It is designed to introduce effective teaching strategies that are appropriate with soccer players. Implementing these methods will not only improve lessons planning, but develop skills of a player.

Establishing Objectives

The first aim of lesson preparation is to determine desired tasks or outcomes; commonly referred as objectives. Objectives are critical in lesson construction. They delineate what should be accomplished and help outline specific activities that teach what is intended to be learned.

Generally, educational outcomes (objective) are arranged in three behavioral domains: psychomotor, cognitive, and affective. The psychomotor domain consists of physical and motor abilities. It involves the movement and application of a technique or skill. Here are examples: (At the end of this lesson the player will)

1. properly shoot and score with the instep;
2. moving to open space after a pass; and
3. successfully tackling the ball from an opponent.

The second domain is cognitive functions. This includes the intellectual thought processes that occurs during play. Illustrations for this include:

1. knowing when to execute an overlapping run;
2. when to commit to a tackle; and
3. explaining the rules of the game.

The final behavioral domain is the affective domain. This area includes aspects related to feelings, attitudes, self-concept, and social interaction. Examples include:

1. successfully working with a partner;
2. demonstrating good sportsmanship during play; and
3. encouraging others in practice.

Photo 2.1

The three domains intersect in the development of students. They are not independent agents designed to be treated separately. During lesson construction and implementation, consistently reinforce learning in each domain. Take advantage of the social and cognitive situations that occur during play. When players become upset with a partner, reinforce the desired outcomes within the affective domain. If a large portion of your class misunderstands a basic tactical move, list it as an objective that needs to be learned in the next lesson.

When objectives are established in each domain, they should be addressed in the lesson and to the students. For the lesson, they supply a blueprint in direction. This is helpful to the instructor. To the class, the objectives provide an understanding in the purpose and reason for the lesson. This is valuable to the student.

Instructional Strategies

The teaching of soccer skills and strategies can be challenging. All instructors have struggled at one time with what to say or do with inexperienced players. Frustration can easily occur. Yet, this is not due to the inability of the player, but often the instructor. To help remember three simple instructional strategies when teaching a new technique or tactic the instructor should: keep it simple, be brief, and maintain one focus at a time.

Keep it simple refers to the amount of information you provide a player. For example, when working on the instep drive, reinforce just one or two concepts at a time. Often instructors will tell a student to contact the center portion of ball, ensure non-kicking foot is parallel to ball during contact, keep your head down and steady with eyes on ball, and continue an upward movement with the kicking leg after contact. This is too much information to provide students at one time. Break it down. Develop one or at most two major aspects at a time. Once students have learned to position the non-kicking foot parallel to the ball during contact, then teach about the follow through. When the player is learning a new concept, he/she is thinking about each step of the process. If there is too much information, some will become lost. Breaking down the skill into parts will not only increase understanding and reinforce proper technique, but educate the player on the importance of each step.

Another component to remember is "be brief." When verbalizing a movement to players be specific and to the point. Often, with new instructors, concepts are overstated and generalized. When introducing a new tactic, discuss the main points, don't try to impress with fancy terms. Make the statement and move them to the field. If something was not understood, reinforce the objective with specific terminology.

The third concept to remember is maintaining one focus at a time. Some instructors have a tendency to teach away from the intended focus. For example, consider the instructor who is working to improve tackling skills. The focus of the drill is proper positioning before the tackle. As the drill progresses, the instructor begins to coach and make comments about aspects of attack. When this occurs, players are redirected in their thinking. At one point, they were concentrating on defensive positioning. Now they are thinking about attack. The focus has been lost. Instructors must maintain their focus in order to accomplish their objective. When they do this, learning and performance is enhanced.

Demonstrating New Tasks

Demonstrating will always be a critical part of learning strategies of soccer. Verbal explanations are helpful, but witnessing how to perform a task is invaluable. When a player can see what is expected he/she will comprehend more information. This is especially true when learning a skill for the first time. There are several components associated with demonstration, and each are important to the instructor. As developed by Graham (1992), they include: location of demonstration, whole and part demonstration, normal and slow demonstration, verbal focus, and checking for understanding.

Location for Demonstration

When working with large groups of players, it is essential that all can see during the demonstration. Correct those out-of-position. You should be able to eye each player and each player should eye you. Stand so the sun is in your eyes, not the players. This can be very disturbing. Always remember that many distraction can be avoided with proper location.

Whole/Part

When a player is learning a technique for the first time, it is important to show the entire movement. This allows the player to see each phase. If teaching the thigh trap, demonstrate (use yourself or a skillful player) the entire action from body positioning, to raising the thigh, receiving the ball, then allowing it to fall to the ground. Once the entire movement is viewed, the instructor can break it down into parts. Obviously, this would depend on the groups skill level. Be prepared to adjust.

Normal/Slow

Graham (1992) indicated that, as with the whole and part, sometimes players need to see the skill at normal speed; other times it helps to slow it down. This will depend on what technique you are teaching. When a new and challenging technique is introduced, a player needs to view the entire method at its normal speed. Players will better comprehend a task if introduced in its natural state. At this point, the instructor can slow down the demonstration and teach the individual parts.

Verbal Focus of the Instructor

When demonstrating a technique it is important to guide the player through the learning process. It will reinforce key points and help ensure the method is understood. This is done by providing a verbal focus. Tell the player what to look for, emphasize specific aspects of the movement, and reinforce proper execution. For example, when introducing the inside-of-the-foot trap, during the demonstration ask players "where the ball contacts the foot," or "how is the body positioned," and "the role of non-kicking foot." By making reference to these actions, you are guiding the player through the learning process. At any point you can stop and reinforce a critical point.

Checking for Understanding

One assumption incorrectly made by many instructors is that once the technique has been explained or demonstrated it is has been learned. Unfortunately this is not true. Frequently, after a thorough description, a student can still be uncertain how to perform the task. This is why instructors need to "check for understanding."

Photo 2.2

There are several ways to accomplished this. One way is to ask the group to perform the technique without a ball, then quickly scan the class. Was there a person who performed the task differently? Did the executions all see appropriate? Another method is to demonstrate the skill incorrectly then ask students what you did wrong. This technique is very effective. It forces the student to analyze each segment of the task. A third way to check for understanding is to ask the group specific questions.

How should you adjust your foot? Where should your eyes be? Explain the proper stance?

Checking for understanding is essential for monitoring learning. Those who teach soccer realize how challenging acquiring motor skills can be. Instructors must ensure that a player understands the purpose and method for completing a task. Those who utilize this method will limit frustrating situations between a player and instructor. Often, the perception is that a player knows what to do and how to do it, but in reality he/she does not.

Providing Feedback

When learning a technique for the first time, or perfecting a technique in a challenging setting, the player will need reinforcement and direction concerning his/her performance. They need to know if the execution is proper and correct. What adjustments should be made. A student also needs encouragement. Effective instructors consistently provide appropriate feedback to class members. Usually, appropriate feedback is classified as specific, simple, and generally positive or neutral (Graham, 1992).

Specific Feedback

Specific feedback pinpoints information on a specific aspect of the movement. Often, feedback is too general. This is when the instructor is not clear in his/her wording. "Great job Jose!" "Kim, wonderful!" What do these statements actually tell the player? What did Jose do that was great? Was it how he kicked the ball, or was it where he ran after the kick? Successful instructors will provide feedback that leads a player to change an inappropriate action to an appropriate action. Examples of specific feedback include:

1. "John, follow through in the direction of the target."
2. "Heidi, toe down."
3. "Great job, you contacted the center portion of the ball."
4. "Jose, good overlapping run."
5. "Terisa, move to the open space."

Simple Feedback

Another consideration in giving feedback is the complexity. How much information should the instructor provide. What do I include? Sometimes, feedback incorporates too much information to process. Successful instructors will attempt to supply information related to one learning component. This is called simple feedback. Here are some examples of simple feedback:

1. "Gary, follow through."
2. "Eyes on ball."
3. "Follow pass, Rick."
4. "Peggy, support."
5. "Keep head up."

Simple feedback is stated quickly. It targets the need and reinforces the desired outcome with a few words. Often, feedback is generalized and complex. Processing too much information can be difficult. When the instructor provides specific and simple feedback, the player will be clear on how he/she should alter his/her performance.

Positive or Neutral Feedback

Constructive feedback will be more effective if placed in a positive or neutral context. Instructors of physical activities have a tendency to be negative. A remark such as, "what in the world are you doing," not only provides limited help, but creates a negative environment. To motivate and efficiently move a player from inappropriate executions to appropriate ones, provide positive or neutral feedback that is simple and specific. Examples include:

1. "Great job, your tackle was perfect."
2. "Cindy, good move to the left."
3. "Gary, your positioning was correct on that series."
4. "Good eye contact, Susan."
5. "Mark, move forward."

Feedback is an important component to the development of any soccer player. The ability of the player will not matter. All need feedback. Successful instructors who quickly and accurately reinforce the desired technique of tactical move promote learning. When a player comprehends the favorable outcome, changes can begin to occur. This comes from feedback. If uncertain about the application of a move, positive reinforcement will motivate the player to continue to practice.

The Development of the Lesson

Lesson planning is an intricate part of successful soccer instruction. With proper lesson preparation, the instructor will present an organized plan designed to develop and enhance learning. When an instructor enters the field with little direction, disorganization arises. Results can be frustrating for both instructor and player. Instructors can make an estimated 200 decisions every few minutes while teaching. Appropriate planning will enhance instruction and promote the learning of objectives.

Critical Elements of the Lesson

Most lessons will include five critical elements. Each component will progressively follow the other in a logical sequence. Lessons are intended to be developmental. This implies that each component of the lesson will build upon itself. For example, the second practice activity in the body of the lesson should prepare learners for the next challenging activity. The warm-up must also be developmental. If the instructor intends to introduce tackling skills, the warm-up should prepare the muscles to be used during the drills.

As mentioned previously, for a lesson to be successful, the instructor must first establish the objectives. They outline the purpose of the lesson. Will the lesson develop a specific technique, or introduce a new tactic? The objectives delineate intended outcomes of the lesson. At this point, the instructor can formulate a series of activities designed to meet the intended outcomes. This series constitutes the lesson which involves five critical elements. They include:

1. introductory activity,
2. anticipatory set,
3. demonstration,
4. practice activities,
5. closure and review.

Photo 2.3

Each component is centered around the objective(s) of the day. Once the instructor has determined the desired player outcomes, the lesson can be easily and properly formulated. It is understood that every component will not be utilized each and every day. At times the instructor might not demonstrate a new skill because the focus is to review and develop skills already practiced. While this is known, it is necessary for the instructor to be familiar with each component. Instructors are also encouraged to implement and modify according to individual classroom and instructional needs.

Introductory Activity

Most players who enter the field or gym are ready to be active. Often, the last thing they want to do is sit down and listen to the instructor. An instant activity is one way to alleviate this problem. When players arrive at the field, they should be encouraged to immediately participate in a predetermined activity. This activity generally lasts 3 to 5 minutes and is intended to serve two purposes. The first is to provide a warm-up opportunity. It can also serve as a review for the previous lesson or introduce the players to a new objective(s).

Examples of the instant activity could include passing a ball to partner using both feet; dribbling a ball within a confined space interjecting creative feinting moves; juggling the ball by oneself or with a partner; participating in a 2 vs. 2 keep away game. These activities will fulfill the need to be instantly involved with movement, review key points of previous lessons, and prepare players for learning.

Anticipatory Set

Anticipatory set is designed to perform many functions. It is more than simply stating what players will be doing. The Anticipatory set is utilized as a motivational tool, one that involves the excitement of participation. Often, a player will come with limited personal enthusiasm. This can result from the inability to see the purpose of a specific task. The anticipatory set delineates what will occur and why it is beneficial to his/her development. It is intended to provoke the interest of players so they become eager to practice and get involved. Two examples include:

"The other day we worked on penetrating the defense. Can you explain the purpose of this? Once you find yourself in front of the goal, you need to learn how to turn with the ball and find the corner of the net. Today we will be working on quick turns and shooting far post."

16

"What is the critical element of body positioning on defense? Why is it important? Today we are going to work on defending the attacker and keeping him/her from turning toward the goal."

"When you shoot on goal, does the ball ever go over or wide of the goal? Does it lack in power and velocity? Today we are going to practice the proper technique of the shooting with the instep. With successful practice, you will see improvement in the accuracy of your shot."

Demonstration

As previously discussed, demonstration refers to visually portraying how to perform a specific movement or action. Many instructors rely heavily on verbal information when teaching skills. This may cause miscommunication between the player and instructor. Having a clear understanding of what a instructor wants a player to perform is essential for success. Instructors need to physically demonstrate the skill. This can be accomplished in two ways. First, using a player or players to demonstrate. Often, an instructor is not comfortable demonstrating a particular skill. This is the time to select a player who can successfully perform the task. It also allows the instructor to provide
verbal feedback while the skill is being executed. If not appropriate, a second method is simply demonstrate the skill as an individual performing a given task.

Photo 2.4

Practice

The fourth component of a lesson is the actual production and practice of techniques or skills. This section is centered around the chosen objectives established by the instructor. During this phase, the player is given the opportunity to perform a desired movement sequence.

The first step is for the instructor to select the appropriate activities to be practiced. These activities should be patterned after the experience and abilities of the player. Once the activities are chosen, the instructor will establish the methods by which to organize the learning environment. This may include practice sessions in individual, pairs, or large group settings.

Participation in each activity is also very important in terms of development and maintaining interest. Instructors are encouraged to limit all waiting if possible. If forced to have lines, limit the lines to two or three players. This will increase time on task, promote player involvement, and intensity enjoyment.

Another important factor when dealing with effective participation is the transition from one activity to another. This transition must be carefully planned in order to maximize time on task. Instructors are encouraged to formulate a graduated learning experience. As the lesson progresses and skills develop, successful instructors increase the challenge of the task. This will help refine the technique, and improve performance. Likewise, if players are not effective at performing at certain skill levels, instructors should modify the activity. Ensuring success while maintaining a certain level of challenge creates a positive outcome.

Closure and Review

It is important for the instructor to end a class with a formal type of closure. This is the time to review what has been taught, and check for player understanding. During closure a instructor can receive excellent feedback from players. Discovering what was understood, liked and disliked, is helpful in planning process.

The closure can also involve a cool down. Often, soccer lessons are aerobic in nature. When players have engaged in intense practice activities, jogging a few laps around the gym and stretching warm muscles help reduce delayed muscle soreness after exercise. The cool-down will also help the cardiovascular system. During strenuous activity the heart pumps large amounts of blood to working muscles. The blood returns to the heart by the muscles squeezing the veins. If activity is stopped too quickly, the blood is left in the muscles and has trouble going back to the heart. This may cause dizziness which might lead to passing out. Passing a ball to a partner, or a slow jog will prevent the problem and slow the heart down.

Sample Lessons

Sample Lesson Number One

Focus: Passing with both feet

Objectives: During this lesson the player will:

1. pass with the inside-of-the-foot and instep with both feet.
2. consistently pass the ball on the ground with both feet.
3. encourage a partner.
4. make the proper decision about which foot to use when passing.

Materials / Equipment:

1. soccer balls (one for every two players)
2. cones (10)

Safety Tips:

* check field for holes, glass, or hidden equipment

Lesson Activities

(1) *Introductory Activity*

Pass a ball between partners while jogging around half the field. Instructor encourages creative movements and feinting skills. Object is to maintain possession while not touching another pair or their ball. Request players use both feet.

(2) *Anticipatory Set*

Was it challenging to use both feet while moving around the field? After doing that activity did you sense a need to use both feet? Why or why not? Today we will be working on improving your effectiveness of both feet. This will be done in a variety of drills using the instep or inside-of-the-foot as the dominate passing methods.

(3) *Demonstration*

Position two players with one ball in front of the group to demonstrate. Instruct the players to pass with both feet between themselves using the inside-of-the-foot and instep. As they pass, verbalize the body position, leg action, and contact point on the ball. After several combinations using both passing techniques, have the class get a ball and pair up. After getting a partner and ball, they can begin.

(4) *Practice Activities*

a. Two-touch passing with the non-dominate foot to a partner five yards away with the inside-of-the-foot and instep.
b. Extend the distance to ten yards.
c. Alternate using left and right foot after each pass.
d. Decrease the distance to five yards and enforce one-touch passing with both feet.
e. Extend the distance to ten yards with one-touch passing with both feet.
f. Add the instep after 80 percent of the class is successful.
g. In a grid area of 20x20, have four players and two balls two-touch passing between themselves. Call out the name of the person you are passing to so one player does not receive two balls at the same time.
h. Within the same grid, create a 3v1 situation. Require the attackers to only use their weak foot. If ball is taken by defender, the player who lost the ball becomes the next defender.
i. If a group is very successful, limit attackers to two-touches.
j. Continue to alter the drill by limiting the attackers to one-touch.
k. Within the same grid, bring over a second group and create a 4v4 situation. Make one three yard goal at each end line. Require quick one-two touch passing combinations using both feet. Objective is to develop an attack and score a goal by rolling it between the two markers.

(5) *Closure and Review*

a. Juggling ball with partner.
b. After juggling, bring the group in. Ask the importance of passing with both feet. Explain what the next lesson will involve.

Sample Lesson Number Two

Focus: Shielding

Objectives: At the end of the lesson the player will:

1. demonstrate how to place their body between the ball and opponent.
2. sufficiently keep the ball from the defender while searching for a open teammate.
3. explain the proper method of shielding.
4. motivate a partner to work hard.

Materials/Equipment:

1. soccer balls (one ball for every two players)
2. cones (10)

Safety Tips:

1. Check the field for holes, misplaced equipment, or any danger spots.
2. Partners should be paired by age, experience, and maturity.

Lesson Activities

(1) *Introductory Activity* (fast footwork activities)

Each player will get a ball and one partner. The instructor will move the partners through a series of fast footwork activities. Partners switch after 30 seconds. Each activity last one minute.

a. Jump over ball side to side.
b. Tap ball between feet, stay on toes.
c. Alterantly tap top of ball with sole of left than right foot.
d. Draw ball toward body with sole of one foot, push forward with instep of same foot, than draw ball to Body with opposite foot. Continue alternating sequence for 30 seconds.

(2) *Anticipatory Set*

Have you ever found yourself in a position when a defender is on your back and you believe there is no where to go? What happens when you feel pressure from a defender bearing down upon you? Today we are going to discuss how to protect the ball from defenders. We will practice keeping our heads up in order to locate and pass to a teammate.

(3) *Demonstration*

Ask a player to come and demonstrate with you. Position yourself between the player and the ball. Assume a couched position with a low center of gravity. One foot is for support and the other is placed on the ball. Keep your body between the ball and opponent. Ask the defender to slowly move in and attempt to steal the ball. In slow motion show how you adjust your body to compensate for the movements of the defender. Now have two players come and demonstrate the skill. As they are adjusting and moving make verbal comments about the technique.

(4) *Practice Activities*

a. have each player get a partner with one ball between them. (make sure they are appropriately paired) Practice taking turns, at a slow pace, shielding the ball. Switch often.
b. As partners gain confidence, increase the pressure and challenge.
c. See if the partners can keep the ball for five consecutive seconds. Do this activity several times.
d. Place the partners with one ball between them in a 30x30 grid area. At the signal, one player attempts to keep the ball from the other for 15 to 20 seconds. They can move anywhere within the grid. At the whistle, the player with the ball wins and receives one point. If the ball is out-of-bounds when the whistle is blown, no points are awarded. Now the player who started with the ball becomes the defender and the drill continues.
e. Place 6 players with balls and 4 defenders in the 30x30 grid. Upon a signal, the defenders attempt to steal a ball from any attacker. Ball carriers can move anywhere within the grid. If a ball is stolen, the attacker becomes a defender and defender becomes attacker.
f. Within the grid, develop a 5v5 situation with small goals placed at the end lines. Play a small sided game with shielding and keeping the head up as the focus. Work for short, controlled one and two-touch passing combinations.

(5) *Closure and Review*

Why is it important to develop shielding skills? Have someone demonstrate the skill. What do you see about the body positioning? Introduce the next days lessons.

Chapter Three

Techniques of Passing

Introduction

When a team gains possession of the ball each player on that team is on attack. The positioning, movement, and attitudes of the players will determine if the team will score or lose possession. Proper execution of passing, trapping, and shooting is essential for success in soccer. The instructor is responsible for building a solid technical foundation for each player in these basic skills of attack. Without the proper knowledge and capabilities to perform these skills, consistency and achievement during game situations will be limited. One critical aspect of attack is passing. Consistent passing with control and accuracy will make teams successful. The four basic passing techniques a player must master include the inside-of-foot pass, outside-of-foot pass, the chip pass, and instep pass.

This chapter outlines each method and includes a list of specific teaching points and photos. Common faults and suggested corrections will be highlighted. Drills designed to improve and lead a player to develop in each passing technique will also be covered. The roles for the instructor and player are presented to assist in the application of each drill.

Passing with the Inside-of-the-Foot

The most frequent pass a player executes when moving the ball short distances is the inside-of-the-foot pass. This technique is considered the foundation for maintaining ball possession while creating passing combinations which lead to goals. It is the most accurate passing method when the target is less than 20 yards away.

Teaching points for Passing with the Inside-of-the-Foot

1. The non-kicking foot is placed along side the ball during ball contact; toes should be pointing toward the target.
2. The leg of the non-kicking foot should be bent slightly.
3. Shoulders should be square and facing the target.
4. Head down and steady with eyes on the ball.

5. The kicking leg is moved back behind the body and slightly bent with the kicking foot turned about 90 degrees; the inside of the foot is facing the ball.
6. It is essential for the ankle of the kicking foot to be rigid and stiff; this will ensure a firm contact.
7. To keep the ball on the ground, strike at center portion of the ball.
8. After contacting the ball, a smooth and complete follow through in the direction of the target will lead to an accurate pass.

Photos 3.1 - 3.2

Common Faults and Corrections

Fault

Ball lacks pace or speed.

Corrections

1. Ankle not rigid or stiff.
2. Bring kicking leg further back to increase the length of the swing.
3. Foot contact too high on the ball.

Fault

Pass lacks accuracy.

Corrections

1. The toes of non-kicking foot should be pointed toward the target.
2. The shoulders need to be squared toward target.
3. The angle of kicking foot should be 90 degrees at the moment of contact.
4. Eyes should be on the ball with head steady.
5. Kicking leg might be too rigid with the toes pointing down.

Fault

Ball rises in the air.

Corrections

1. Kicking foot should contact the middle portion of the ball.
2. Trunk of body might be leaning back during ball contact.
3. The passer might be reaching to contact the ball; make sure the player is in a comfortable position during contact.

Drills to Develop Passing with the Inside–of–the–Foot

Each drill is designed for a player to properly execute the inside-of-the-foot pass. As the player begins to master the pass, increase the distance by moving the player further apart from his/her partner, or have the player utilize both feet. This will depend upon the situation. When an instructor is incorporating a new technique, allow the player to progress slowly. He/she should first be given the opportunity to comprehend how to execute the pass before placed in a challenging situation. The following six drills follow a progressive, easy to difficult, sequence of experiences.

Drill Number One

Passing to partner: During this drill a player is asked to accurately pass the ball across to a partner using the inside of his/her left or right foot.

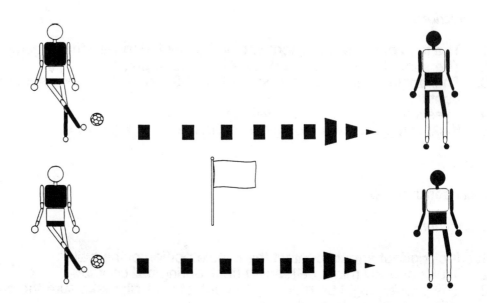

Fig 3.1

Role of the Passer

1. Cognitively (mentally) evaluate the correct body movement and position that will lead to a successful pass.
2. Make a personal adjustment when necessary.
3. Consistently pass the ball to the feet of partner.
4. Increase pace (speed) as partner becomes successful.

Role of Instructor

1. Search for inappropriate applications of the technique and make proper adjustments.
2. Verbally reinforce the emphasis of consistency and accuracy of the pass.
3. Move around and view all players.
4. Increase distance as players become more proficient.
5. Encourage partners to increase the pace of ball as they develop skill.
6. Encourage a player to make his/her partner successful by keeping the ball on the ground and providing accurate passes directed to his/her feet.
7. Challenge a player to apply one touch passing techniques as skill develops in both feet.

Performance Benefits of Passing to Partner

1. Provides a successful situation.
2. Allows enough time for each player to properly execute the technique.
3. Contributes to the success of the player by allowing advancement at his/her own pace.

Drill Number Two

Line Passing: Player (a) positioned in front of a line will pass the ball with the inside-of-the-foot to the player across the line, player (b). After each pass the player will follow his/her pass (running) and line-up in the opposite line. Player (b) will receive, control, and pass the ball back to the line he/she is facing. Player (b) will also follow the pass. The rotation will appear according to the figure below.

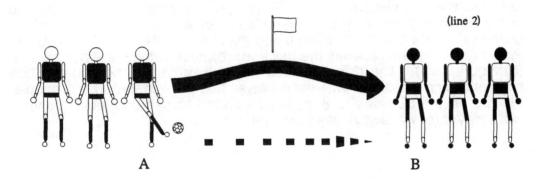

(line 2)

A   B

Fig 3.2

Role of Passer

1. Control the ball before attempting to pass across opposing players.
2. Apply appropriate inside-of-the-foot technique, keeping eyes on the ball while receiving and executing the pass.
3. Attempt to one-touch the ball back to the opposing line as the passer becomes more proficient.
4. Quickly make the pass; run to opposing line while maintaining balance, control, and accuracy.

Role of Instructor

1. Limit six players per group, three to each side. This will increase number of repetitions each player experiences.
2. Encourage the passer to control the ball then execute the pass quickly and accurately.
3. Move around to all groups and provide correctional feedback.
4. Increase the pressure and pace by limiting the groups to four players, two to a side.
5. Request that players return a one-touch pass using the inside of the foot.

Performance Benefits of Line Passing

1. Increases the challenge from drill number one.
2. Requires a player to move and pass.
3. Forces a player to use both feet depending on how the ball is received.

Drill Number Three

Man in the Middle: During this drill two players are separated by 10 to 15 yards, each possessing a ball (players a & b). A third player (c) is placed between the two without a ball. Player (a) will pass the ball, using the inside of his/her foot to player (c). Player (c) will return the ball back to player (a) with a one-touch pass using the inside-of-the-foot (Figure One). Player (c) turns and receives the ball from (b), then returns the ball back to (b)(Figure Two). The drill continues for approximately one minute, then players switch positions until each player has participated in the middle. Players on the outsides (a & b) are reminded to use two-touch passing while player (c) will always use the one-touch pass.

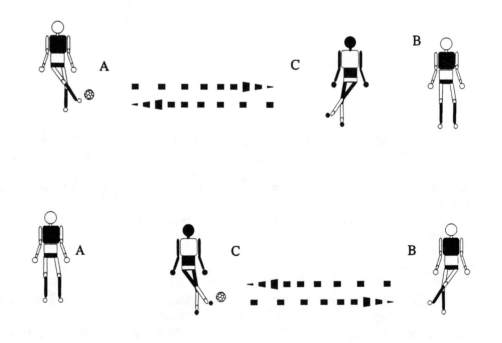

Fig 3.3

Role of Player

1. Challenge the player in the middle by restricting the waiting time.
2. Accurately and consistently pass the ball to the feet and on the ground.
3. Encourage and reinforce the positive results from teammates.

Role of Instructor

1. Require quick release of ball.
2. Reinforce proper technique, especially if players are exhausted.
3. Move the outside players back or forward depending on the success of the man in the middle.
4. Encourage players to bear their body weight on the balls of their feet.
5. Inspire a player to keep eyes on ball and on partner while receiving and executing passes.
6. Depending on the success of a particular group, increase the challenge by requesting that all players utilize the one-touch pass.

Performance Benefits of Man in the Middle

1. Increases the pressure and develops a quick reaction and adjustment to various passes.
2. Increases concentration and passing accuracy.
3. Teaches a player to maintain balance and body control while controlling and passing the ball in a pressure situation.

Drill Number Four

Wall passing (Six-touch): To construct this drill, the instructor must place three players (Line-A) in line one facing another group of three players (line-C) that are positioned 15 to 20 yards away. One player (b) will be placed in the middle of the two lines and stationed about 15 yards back. The passing combination will play out as follows: Player (a) will pass the ball (pass-1) to player (b). Player (b) will one-touch the ball back (pass-2) to (a) who is running toward line two. Player (a) will control the ball from (b) and pass it (pass-3) to player (c) who is positioned at the front of line two. Once player (a) passes the ball to player (c) he/she will line-up at the back of line two. Player (c) will pass (pass-4) in the same configuration as (a) and conclude by lining-up behind line one. The drill will continue as long as necessary. Minor adjustments in the distances and angles of players may be required.

30

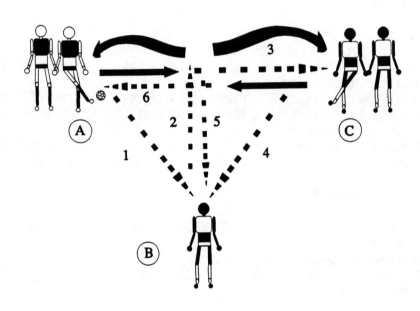

Fig 3.4

Role of Player

1. Review various passing angles and make appropriate adjustments.
2. Quickly move to target area while maintaining control and balance.
3. Anticipate a player's position and successfully pass to partner's feet.
4. Verbally encourage team work and accurate passing to develop a successful combination of six passes with an emphasis placed on passing with the inside-of-the-foot.

Role of Instructor

1. Reinforce a quick ball release.
2. Encourage the player to strive for consistency and efficiency.
3. Watch for proper approach, concentration, and control.

Performance Benefits of Six-Touch Passing

1. Requires a player to pass while on the run.
2. Forces a player to accurately adjust to the various passing angles.

3. Reinforces rapid movements with quick release of the ball while maintaining stability and control.
4. Builds wall passing tactics which occur during game situations.

Drill Number Five

Four vs. One Outside the Grid: To arrange this drill the instructor will need to build a 10x10 yard grid marked by cones or corner flags. Five players are needed. Four players are placed outside the grid. One defender will be placed in the middle. Players on the outside can move along the 10 yard line to position themselves for a pass; movement must be continuous. The instructor should stress the inside-of-the-foot pass throughout this drill. The objective of the drill is to have the outside players maintain possession while passing between themselves. The defender is actively attempting to steal the ball.

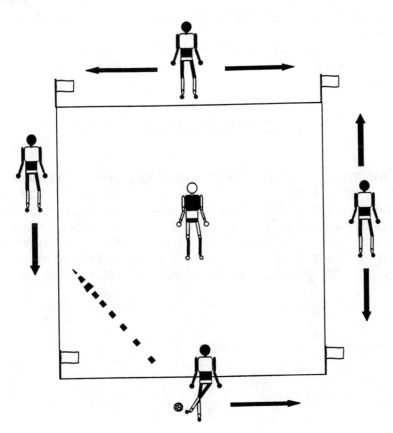

Fig 3.5

Role of Passer

1. Emphasis is placed on composure and control.
2. Observe the movements and actions of defender when passing to teammates.
3. Consistently change passing direction.
4. Disguise intentions and make continual movements between flags.

Role of Instructor

1. Reinforce a quick release after controlling the ball.
2. Provide positive feedback to a player who passes to his/her teammates with the most space.
3. Encourage one-touch passing.
4. Increase the pressure by adding a second defender to the middle after the outside players consistently maintain possession.

Performance Benefits of Four vs. One Outside the Grid

1. Requires a player to determine passing angles while avoiding defender(s).
2. Forces a player to move and generate open passing angles.
3. Encourages a player to develop one-touch passing skills with accuracy.

Drill Number Six

Three vs. One Inside the Grid: Three attacking players are placed inside a 10x10 grid. One defender is positioned in the middle of the attacking players. The object is for the attacking players to maintain ball possession and create open spaces without allowing the defender to intercept or block a pass. Space will equal time, time to pass, shoot, or move the ball. Creating this space is a challenge and the player needs to learn the initial concept of how to generate open space for teammates in attacking situations.

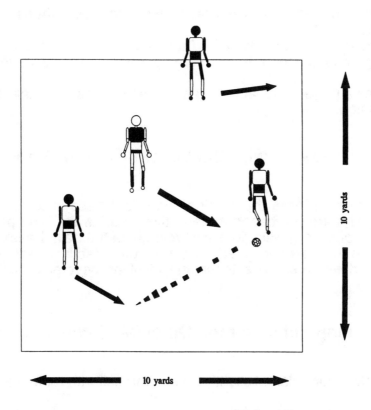

Fig. 3.6

Role of Passer

1. Move to open space.
2. Disguise intentions.
3. Execute one-touch passing with inside-of-the-foot.

Role of Instructor

1. Emphasize a quick ball release and rapid movements to open spaces within the grid area.
2. Reinforce the concept of improvision, which refers to the creative and deceptive movements an attacker initiates to open-up spaces. These actions are designed to place a defender(s) out of position and off balance.
3. As attackers increase in proficiency and produce creative passing combinations with movement, add a second defender to the grid area and encourage attackers to "split the defenders" and make passes between the two opposing players.

Performance Benefits of Three vs. One Inside the Grid

1. Requires a player to think where and when to move when he/she does not have the ball.
2. Teaches a player to disguise his/her intentions in order to increase the passing options and generate more space and/or time to work the ball.
3. Requires a player to locate or create open spaces and maintain possession.

Passing with the Outside-of-the-Foot

A player who utilizes the outside-of-the-foot pass is usually targeting teammates who are positioned three to five yards away. The pass utilizes a quick snap of the leg yielding a swift release of the ball. Passing with the outside-of-the-foot is often used as a deceptive tactic when confronting one or two defenders. The technique involves several critical teaching points.

Teaching Points for the Outside-of-the-Foot Pass

1. Non-kicking foot placed slightly behind the ball with toes pointing forward.
2. Body is upright, eyes on ball.
3. The calf of kicking leg is pulled back with toes pointed down and ankle firm.
4. Ball contact is on side of foot slightly below toes.
5. Head is down and steady; eyes on ball.
6. The swing of the kicking leg should be a quick strike, almost a snap, and concluding with a follow through.

Photos 3.3 - 3.4

Common Faults and Corrections

Fault

Pass lacks speed.

Corrections

1. Ankle must be rigid
2. Move the foot through the ball after contact.

Fault

Ball is driven into the ground.

Corrections

1. Move non-kicking foot slightly behind the ball.
2. Outside of foot needs to contact the center portion of the ball.
3. Keep eyes on ball.

Fault

Ball rises off the ground.

Corrections

1. Lean body slightly forward.
2. Contact the center portion of the ball.
3. Kicking leg is placed behind the ball at the point of contact.

Fault

Ball curves (spins) away from target.

Correction

Strike ball with firm instantaneous contact at the mid-line, do not roll foot around ball.

Drills to Develop Passing with Outside–of–the–Foot

Drill Number One

Z Passing: Players are lined-up 10 to 15 yards apart. One ball is given to two players. At the signal, the first player will pass the ball ahead to his/her partner who is running in a straight line down the field. After controlling the ball, the receiving player will return the ball back to the partner who is moving down the opposite line. They will continue to pass back and forth for a designated distance of 50 to 75 yards. As the front pair begin to move well away from the others, the instructor can send the next pair of players into the drill.

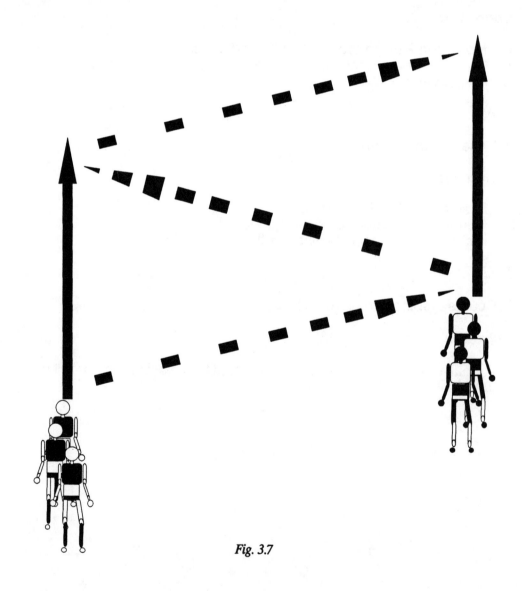

Fig. 3.7

Role of Passer

1. Pass with the outside-of-the-foot to the feet of partner.
2. Continue to move to the end without stopping while controlling and passing with the outside-of-the-foot to partner's feet.
3. Watch partner's movements and actions, anticipate the passing angle, and adjust the speed to ensure an accurate pass.
4. Strike the ball in the center to keep it on the ground.

Role of Instructor

1. Encourage a player to maintain balance and bodily control while executing each pass.
2. Reinforce targeting and hitting the partner's feet.
3. Encourage partners to increase the pace of the ball and speed of the run as they become more proficient.
4. Support the one-touch passing option as partners become efficient.

Performance Benefits of Z Passing

1. Reinforces a player to learn passing angles while passing to a partner on the run.
2. Allows a player the opportunity to perfect the outside of the foot pass in an environment with limited pressure.
3. A player can move at his/her own pace and personally make it more challenging by opting to increase the running speed and/or passing with one or two touches.

Drill Number Two

Circular Passing: One player will stand with a ball 3 to 5 yards from a partner. When the whistle is blown the ball carrier will run in a circular motion around a stationary player (player in the middle). The stationary player will return the pass to the feet of the moving player. The moving player will one-touch the ball back to the stationary player, and the drill continues in this fashion. As the moving player continues to move around the stationary player, he/she is receiving a pass and one-touching the ball back to the stationary player with the outside foot.

38

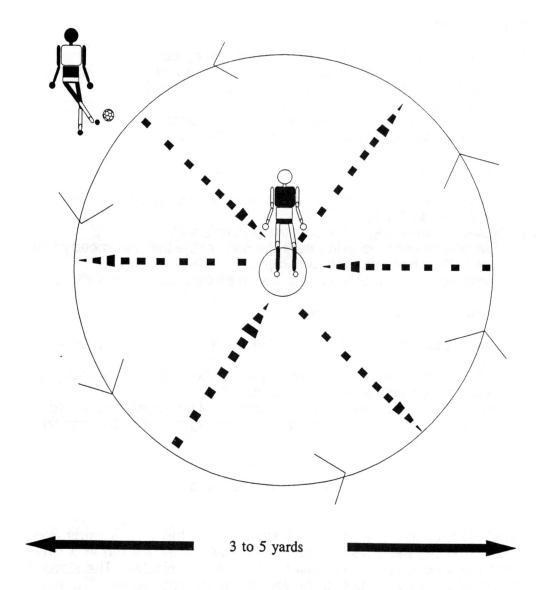

3 to 5 yards

Fig. 3.8

Role of Passer

1. Stationary player will utilize either one or two-touch passing techniques depending on the angle of the receiving pass.
2. Moving player is asked to increase the pace as he/she becomes proficient with a properly executed outside-of-the-foot pass.
3. Stationary player is to verbally encourage and motivate the moving player.
4. Both players should strike the ball in the center portion to keep it on the ground.

Role of Instructor

1. Change the direction of the moving player every 20 to 30 seconds to develop coordination in both feet.
2. Move around to all passing groups and provide feedback to each player.
3. Focus on appropriate applications and make corrections.

Performance Benefits of Circular Passing

1. Develops the skills of targeting a moving player with a designated pass.
2. Reinforces appropriate technique while strengthening one-touch and two-touch passing methods in both feet.
3. Increases cardiovascular endurance and muscular strength.

Drill Number Three

Quad Passing: During this drill, arrange four players on the outside of a 10 x 10 yard grid. Players are asked to pass a ball with the outside of the foot to any player within their group. Players are encouraged to move along their line of the grid while applying creative and deceptive moves with the ball. As players become comfortable with movements, the instructor adds a second ball to each group of four. Emphasis is placed on passing with the outside-of-the-foot.

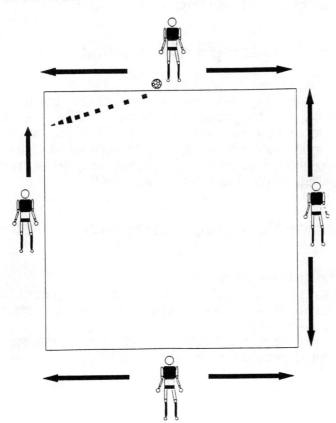

Role of Passer

1. Develop creative and deceptive moves with the ball while passing with the outside-of-the-foot to partners in the grid.
2. Concentrate; who has the ball and anticipate who will receive a ball so a player is not passed two balls at the same time.
3. Consistently change passing directions and combinations within the group.
4. Communicate with partner before a pass takes place.

Role of Instructor

1. Increase or decrease the grid area depending on success of the players.
2. Add the second ball when the group consistently executes various passing combinations with creativity and imagination.
3. Encourage and reinforce consistent movement of players around the grid.

Performance Benefits of Quad Passing

1. Requires a player to develop creative and deceptive passing combinations.
2. Reinforces the development of both feet.
3. Demands concentration; who and when to make a pass.
4. Develops one-touch and two-touch passing skills.

Passing with the Instep

The most powerful pass that can be generated is the instep or instep drive. A player will use the instep to split the defense with a quick and forceful pass or to make a shot on goal from 20 to 25 yards away. This passing technique is more difficult to master compared to the outside-of-the-foot or inside-of-the-foot pass. The instep is a small hitting surface, thus requiring perfect contact to maintain accuracy.

Teaching Points for Passing with the Instep

1. Approach the ball straight on.
2. The non-kicking foot is placed beside the ball during contact.
3. The leg of the non-kicking foot is slightly bent and toes are pointing in the direction of the target.
4. The head should be down and steady with eyes on the ball.
5. The kicking leg is brought back behind the body.

6. Arm opposite of kicking leg is brought forward and slightly across the body.
7. The ankle of the kicking leg is rigid and placed in the plantar flexed position.
8. The ball is contacted with the flat surface of the foot and the toes of the kicking foot are pointed down.
9. Strike the ball in the center portion to keep it on the ground.
10. The kicking leg should follow through in the direction of the target.

Photos 3.5 - 3.6

Common Faults and Corrections

Fault

Ball lacks pace or speed

Corrections

1. Ankle needs to be firm or rigid.
2. Contact the ball in the center; foot might be hitting too high on the ball forcing it into the ground.

Fault

Ball lacks accuracy.

Corrections

1. Contact center of ball.
2. The toes of the non-kicking foot should be pointed toward target.
3. Eyes need to be on the ball before and during contact.

Fault

Ball spins away from target.

Corrections

1. Strike the center of the ball. If struck on the left or right side it will cause a spinning motion and move away from the target.
2. Make sure the arm opposite the kicking leg is moved forward and positioned slightly across the body (if chest is squared toward target, shot will pull to the side.)

Fault

Ball rises in the air.

Corrections

1. Foot of kicking leg is turned up, not flat or in plantar position with toes pointing down.
2. Ball is struck below its mid-line.
3. Body should be forward with head down. Do not lean back.

Drills for Passing with the Instep

The instep is a very effective technique for long powerful passes down field. The fullback positioned near the goal uses this technique to counter attack, targeting a long pass down field to an on-rushing striker or winger. Midfield players utilize this technique to make long passes down the flanks. The drills for this section are designed to introduce a player to use this method during various passing situations. Additional drills for shooting with the instep are provided in chapter five.

Drill Number One

Single Man Pressure Passing: Two players (a & b) stand across from each other approximately 5 to 10 yards apart. Positioned 15 to 20 yards away are two corner flags or cones separated by 10 yards. A third player (c) is positioned between the two markers. The sequence will go as follows. Player (c) runs across to a marker, receives and returns a pass from (a), then runs to receive and return a pass from (b). Player (c) will move back and forth from marker to marker receiving and returning passes to and from players (a) and (b). Emphasis is placed on the instep pass.

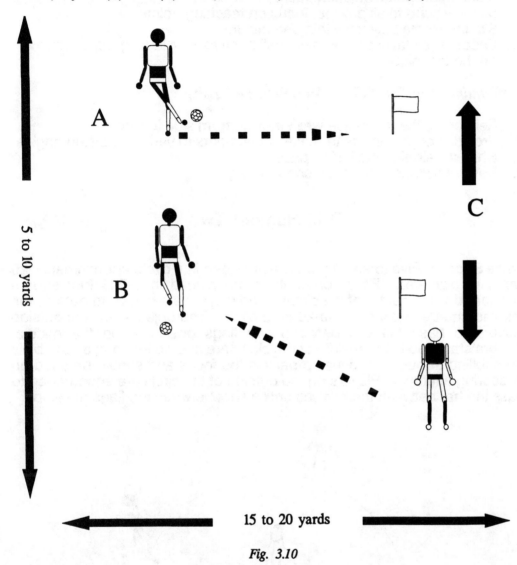

5 to 10 yards

15 to 20 yards

Fig. 3.10

Role of Player

1. Middle player (c) controls a pass and executes the instep pass to the feet of the stationary target, either (a) or (b).
2. Middle player quickly accelerates to receive the ball.
3. Outside players (a & b) increase the pace of ball as the middle player gains proficiency.
4. Outside players release the ball as quickly as possible, depending on the stamina and performance of middle player.
5. Outside players should encourage and motivate the middle player.

Role of Instructor

1. Reinforce the instep; determine why inaccurate passes occur and make appropriate adjustments.
2. Move around to all groups; focus on teaching points.
3. Switch middle players within one minute.
4. Encourage players to increase ball pace as individual groups improve on the technique.

Performance Benefits of Single Man Pressure Passing

1. Reinforces the technique while moving from side to side.
2. Provides opportunities to make adjustments to various passing angles while developing the instep pass.
3. Develops fitness and body competency.

Drill Number Two

Circle Soccer: Five to six players are arranged in a circle approximately 20 yards in diameter. Four corner flags are placed in a 5x5 foot square positioned in the center of the circle. Two players are stationed outside the marked square and inside the 20 yard circle. The object is for the outside players to pass the ball between two flags positioned in the middle. Players stationed in the middle of the circle are attempting to keep the balls from rolling through. The instep pass is the focus and should be used on all scoring attempts. Players on the outside of the circle are encouraged to pass the ball between themselves until a shot between the flags develops.

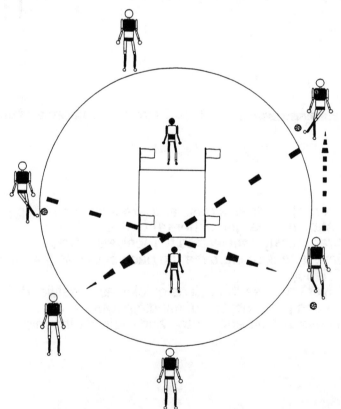

Role of Passer

1. Attempt to place middle players off balance by consistent deception and movement.
2. Quickly receive and release the ball with either a pass or shot.
3. Player needs to position himself/herself to receive a pass that allows a one-touch passing opportunity between the flags.
4. Strike center of ball to keep it on the ground.

Role of Instructor

1. Encourage a quick release. Do not allow a player to keep the ball.
2. Emphasize one-touch passing while focusing on the instep.
3. Watch the application of the instep, reinforce appropriate execution and assurance of accuracy and control.
4. Increase or decrease the circumference of the circle depending on the success of outside players.

Performance Benefits of Circle Soccer

1. Reinforces movement and creativity while attempting to open the defense.
2. Forces a player to properly apply the instep drive without lifting the ball off the ground.
3. Encourages consistent movement and quick release of the ball.

Drill Number Three

Distance Passing: Players are positioned in two lines across from each other. The player with the ball will use the instep to pass across the field to the first player on the opposite side of the field. Once the receiving player controls the pass he/she returns the ball back to the partner who is moving down the opposite side-line. Passing combinations continue down the field. Once the first group of players has moved well away from the others, the second group may begin.

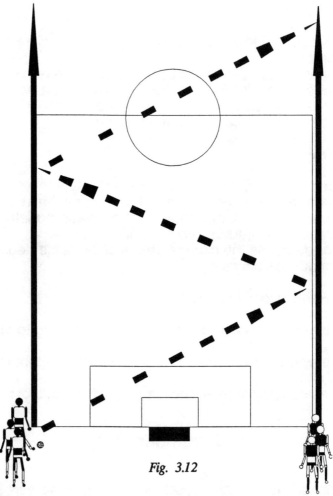

Fig. 3.12

Role of Player

1. Execute a powerful and accurate instep drive to a moving partner.
2. Anticipate where the partner will be and pass to that spot.
3. Move down the field in a quick and controlled manner.

Role of the Instructor

1. Encourage powerful but controlled passes.
2. Watch for speed adjustments in the run and make suggestions when appropriate.
3. Encourage the player to control the ball before attempting to pass.

Performance Benefits of Distance Passing

1. Requires a player to judge the distance and power of a pass and adjust his/her speed and position to properly receive the ball.
2. Forces a player to accurately execute the instep drive a great distance away.
3. Reinforces ball control before making the pass.

The Chip Pass

A player is confronted with situations during play that require a pass in the air. This type of loft pass is called the chip. A player utilizes the chip in a variety of situations for short and long distances. When a defender has opened up space behind him/her, a player can apply the chip to get the ball over the defender and to a teammate. To create the necessary height, the foot contacts the bottom portion of the ball. Approach the ball at an angle and slide the instep of the kicking foot underneath the bottom portion of the ball. This will ensure maximum height. To alter the height and trajectory, modify the approach and location of foot contact to the ball.

Teaching Points for the Chip Pass

1. Approach the ball at a slight angle.
2. Non-kicking foot should be placed slightly behind the ball.
3. Leg on non-kicking foot should be bent at the knee.
4. Kicking leg is drawn back.
5. Head is down and steady with eyes on the ball.
6. Foot of kicking leg is slightly turned-up.
7. Arm opposite of kicking leg is pulled slightly forward.
8. Ankle of kicking foot is rigid.
9. The kicking leg is swept underneath the ball to provide the lifting actions required to raise the ball high in the air.
10. Ball contact is just below the instep on the foot.
11. The kicking leg is moved forward in the direction of the target after ball contact.

Photos 3.7 - 3.8

Fault

Ball does not rise into the air.

Corrections

1. Strike bottom portion of ball close to the ground.
2. Turn ankle slightly up in a cupped position.
3. Ball contact should be at the lower portion of instep, near the toe.

Fault

Ball lacks accuracy.

Corrections

1. Toes of the non-kicking foot need to point toward target.
2. Strike ball at the bottom half in the center. If struck on the sides, the ball will spin away from target.
3. Kicking leg must follow through in the direction of the target.
4. Ankle of kicking foot must be rigid and stiff during ball contact.

Drills Designed to Develop the Chip Pass

Teaching the chip pass is often overshadowed by the inside-of-the-foot or outside-of-the-foot pass, and in some cases even the instep. To master the chip a player is required to understand the technical aspects of this passing method. Numerous repetitions are needed for mastery. It differs from the previously listed passing techniques, and requires many alterations. Reinforce the specific teaching points listed above during each drill.

Drill Number One

Passing to Partner: Player (a) will chip the ball over player (b) and to the feet of player (c). Player (c) is positioned 15 to 20 yards from player (a). Players (a) and (c) will chip back and forth to each other, then rotate with player (b) until all players have the opportunity to be in the middle.

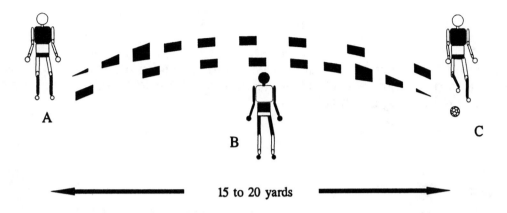

Fig. 3.13

Role of Passer

1. Control ball before attempting to chip over to the target.
2. Glance at target just before striking the ball. Ensure head is down and steady.
3. Eyes on ball before and during ball contact.
4. Attempt to increase the lift of ball with each chip while maintaining accuracy.

Role of Instructor

1. Focus on the execution of the chipping technique. Make adjustments when necessary.
2. Decrease or increase the distance of players depending on success and proficiency.
3. Reinforce control and patience in each player when he/she strikes the ball.
4. As a player becomes successful, allow him/her to increase the pace of the pass.
5. As the entire group becomes successful, have the middle player move in the direction of the passing player to increase the height and challenge of the chip.

Performance Benefits of Passing to Partner

1. Provides a non-stressful environment for players to understand and master the chipping technique.
2. Provides opportunities for players to progress at their own pace.

Drill Number Two

Turn and Chip: Player (a) will receive a short pass from player (b). Player (a) will control, turn, and chip the ball over a marker to an onrushing player (c) who is heading down field.

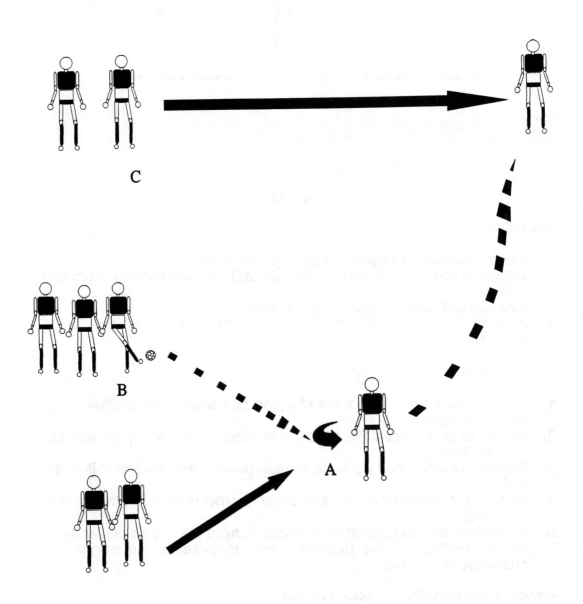

Fig. 3.14

Role of Passer

1. Modify the pace and power of the chip depending on the run of player (c).
2. Player (a) should control the ball first, then turn and chip.
3. Quickly glance at the run of player (c) before attempting the chip. This will ensure proper judgment of the angle and distance of the pass.
4. Player (b) must provide an accurate pass on the ground to increase success of (a).
5. Player (c) must control the speed of the run and make appropriate adjustments to the ball.
6. Player (c), watch, do not run too soon!

Role of the Instructor

1. Observe the proper execution of the chipping technique. Make modification when necessary.
2. Encourage player (a) to turn and release the ball quickly.
3. Modify the situation by having player (c) shoot on a goal.

Performance Benefits of Turn and Chip

1. Encourages a player to judge the speed and angle of a teammate on the run.
2. Requires a player to involve many skills while emphasizing the chip.

Passing with the Head

During the course of a soccer match, a player is often confronted with a ball that is played in the air rather than on the ground. This requires the player to use his/her head rather than other body parts. Passing, shooting, or clearing an area with the head is a vital skill for all players. There are many types of heading techniques. Some require great skill.

Heading the ball requires concentration and proper timing. When preparing to head a ball the player must remember two critical components. First, get to the ball before anyone else. Second, accurately time the run.

To properly execute the technique, a player should bend from the waist, moving the upper trunk back. Eyes should be on the ball with head steady. At the appropriate time, snap the trunk forward and strike the ball with the forehead, just above the eyebrows. Keep eyes open and mouth closed. Move the head into and through the center portion of the ball. Instructors are to remind the player to strike the ball, and not have the ball strike them!

Photos 3.9 - 3.10

There are two other heading methods that are commonly used during a soccer match; the jumping and diving header. They are exciting to watch. Many spectacular goals are scored by players using either techniques.

The Jumping Header

The jumping header is used when a player approaches a ball above the height of his/her head. A player will use this method to clear a ball from a dangerous situation, or when confronting on-rushing opponents of superior numbers. Other one-on-one confrontations requiring the jumping header include shooting on goal, passing to a teammate, or clearing the ball.

Teaching Points for the Jumping Header

1. Eyes on ball.
2. Shoulders square toward target.
3. Both knees bent.
4. Swing arms back to generate upward momentum.
5. Jump up.
6. Arch trunk back while in the air.
7. Neck rigid.
8. Snap trunk forward.
9. Contact ball at forehead, between eyebrows and hairline.
10. Keep eyes open and mouth closed.
11. Drive forehead through the ball.

Photos 3.11 - 3.12

Common Faults and Corrections

Fault

Ball lacks pace and power.

Corrections

1. Snap forward from the upper trunk.
2. Keep neck rigid.
3. Make sure the player strikes the ball and the ball is not striking the player.
4. Strike the ball with the forehead; it is the hardest part of the skull.

Fault

Ball lacks accuracy.

Corrections

1. Keep eyes on ball.
2. Shoulders squared in the direction of the target.
3. Neck rigid.
4. Strike the ball with the forehead, between the eyebrows and hairline.

Fault

Ball is not struck at the highest point of jump.

Corrections

Accomplishing this technique correctly requires practice. Options to help a player master this technique include the following:

1. Be patient before jumping and attempt to accurately judge the height of the ball; work through a trial and error period.
2. Drive both arms up to help increase the height of the jump.
3. Jump early, but not too early; attempt to hang in the air and wait for the ball.

Drills to Develop the Jumping Header

Understanding when to initiate the jumping header is vital for a successful outcome. A player will need to accurately judge the speed and height of the ball. Drills providing a player with various situations and challenges help lead a player to victory.

Drill Number One

Striking a Stationary Ball: One player will hold a ball above his/her head while a partner will attempt to jump and head the held ball. The heading player continues jumping and heading the ball while attempting to knock it out of the hands of partner. After 30 seconds, players switch roles.

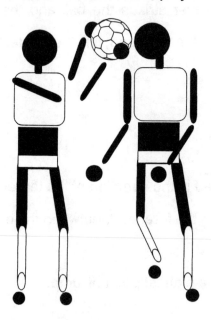

Fig. 3.15

Role of Heading Player

1. Concentrate on appropriate technique while attempting to increase the height of every jump.
2. Keep eyes on ball.
3. Use arms to gain momentum in jumping.
4. Snap upper trunk and make a solid contact on ball with forehead.
5. Continue jumping with two small jumps between each ball striking jump.

Role of Player Holding Ball

1. Hold ball firmly in hands.
2. Adjust the height of the ball as partner gains success.
3. Verbally challenge partner to knock ball out of hands.

Role of Instructor

1. Encourage players to maintain consistency in movement and proper execution of jumping technique.
2. Switch partners periodically.
3. Arrange players by height.

Performance Benefits of Striking a Stationary Ball

1. Reinforces appropriate technique.
2. Develops consistency through many repetitions.
3. Increases muscle and cardiorespiritory fitness.
4. A player identifies the proper movement.

Drill Number Two

Jumping Header to Server: A serving player (positioned 10 to 15 feet from away) will toss a lofted ball for a partner to head. The heading player will return the serve with a jumping header.

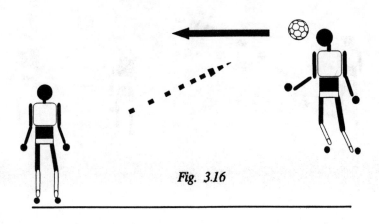

Fig. 3.16

56

Role of Heading Player

1. Accurately time the jump to the lofted ball.
2. Patiently wait for the ball; do not jump too soon.
3. Keep eyes on ball and concentrate throughout the jumping action.
4. Glance at target to place the pass before leaving the ground.
5. Strike through the ball with the forehead implementing a strong snap from the waist.

Role of Serving Player

1. Serve the ball in various distances and heights depending on the success of the partner.
2. Serve a smooth lofted ball, easy to strike, maintaining proper development of the technique.

Role of Instructor

1. Adjust the distance and height of the served ball.
2. Allow serving partner to alter the direction of serve as the player becomes proficient.
3. Alternate partners periodically.

Performance Benefits of Jumping Header to Server

1. A player learns to adjust movements and timing of his/her jump.
2. Increases the accuracy of passing with the jumping header.
3. Perfects the technique in a controlled situation.
4. Requires a player to judge the height and angles of the serve.

Drill Number Three

Beating Defender: One player will toss a ball over a passive defender to the heading partner. The heading player will jump and head the ball over the defender back to the server.

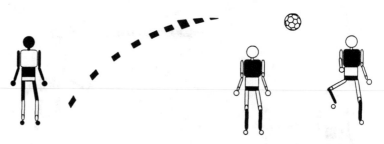

Fig. 3.17

Role of Heading Player

1. Time the jump in relation to the height and speed of the ball.
2. Implement the proper technique while rising above the defender
3. Contact the ball at its highest point without making contact with defender.
4. Eye the target before leaving the feet.
5. Defending player is to maintain a stationary position in front of heading player.

Role of Instructor

1. Encourage a powerful contact on the ball.
2. Watch for the appropriate application of the technique while maintaining the player's focus on accuracy and consistency.
3. Encourage the server to move either to the right or left after each serve to force the heading player to hit the pass to alternating target.
4. Allow the server to move farther back as the heading player develops proficiency.
5. Modify the drill by allowing the passive defender to become more active.
6. Rotate all players until each has the opportunity to head the ball.

Performance Benefits of Beating Defender

1. Forces the heading player to jump above an opponent while controlling the body and executing the proper technique.
2. Encourages heading player to view a target before striking the ball.

Drill Number Four

Heading to Target While Beating Opponent: Player (a) and (b) are attempting to out jump each other and win the ball by heading it to a designated target. Player (a) is trying to head the ball to target (1) while player (b) is going for target (2). The serving player (c) will alter the angle, height, and direction of each serve. Players collect ball and rotate lines after each attempt.

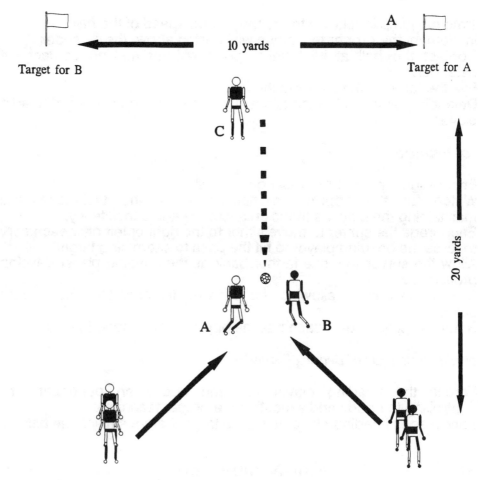

Fig. 3.18

Role of Heading Players

1. Time the jump and be patient; wait for the ball; don't jump too soon.
2. Station body in the proper position before leaving the ground.
3. Challenge for positioning.
4. Eye target before leaving the ground.
5. Apply appropriate method and keep eyes on ball throughout entire attempt.

Role of Instructor

1. Encourage a high lofted serve.
2. Allow the server to place the ball in various directions, not only in the middle of the two challenging for it, but to the sides.
3. Encourage server to loft the ball in front of players forcing them to move.
4. Rotate the servers to allow all the players the opportunity to head the ball.

Performance Benefits of Heading to Target While Beating Opponent

1. Forces a player to challenge for the ball.
2. Requires a player to judge the height, speed, and direction of the ball while being confronted with an opponent.
3. Encourages a player to head toward a target.

The Diving Header

Successful shooting or passing with the diving header requires courage, concentration, and skill. The diving header is exciting to watch and often produces tremendous goals. Many instructors caution their players about this technique, especially in crowded areas on the field. It can be very dangerous. When a player is not careful, he/she can be kicked in the front or back of the head. To ensure safety, instructors should teach the proper techniques and warn of inherent dangers.

Teaching Points for the Diving Header

1. Feet shoulder length apart.
2. Knees bent and weight on balls of feet.
3. Eyes on ball.
4. Arms slightly backward.
5. Head and neck rigid.
6. Dive toward ball and strike it with the forehead, between eyebrows and hairline.
7. Arms move forward to break fall with palms down after contact.
8. Keep eyes open and mouth closed.
9. Break fall with hands; arms extended forward.

Photos 3.13 - 3.15

Common Faults and Corrections

Fault

Ball lacks power and pace.

Corrections

1. Neck rigid; head steady.
2. Contact ball with forehead, below hairline.

Fault

Ball lacks accuracy.

Corrections

1. Glance at target before striking ball.
2. Keep eyes on ball slightly before, during, and after contact.
3. Strike ball with forehead, above hairline.

Drills to Develop Diving Header

Training activities to develop the diving header progress at a slow and controlled pace. Utilization of the appropriate method is essential for safety and success. An instructor must have an awareness of the skill level of his/her players. Adjustments based on experience and maturity should be introduced. All players need to learn the diving header regardless of age; modify the drills to meet the player's needs.

Drill Number One

Heading from the Knees: Player (b) will be positioned on his/her knees. Player (a) will stand 5 to 10 yards away preparing to serve the ball slightly in front of the head of player (b). Player (b) will head the ball with the diving header from the kneeling position. The serving player will toss the ball 5 to 10 times; then switch.

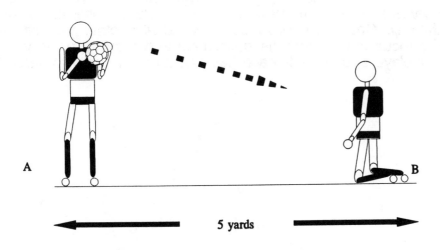

Fig. 3.19

Role of Player

1. Player (b) needs to loft a soft serve at a 35 degree angle to ensure success and proper execution of player (b).
2. Player (a) needs to concentrate and strike the ball with appropriate technique. Remember to break fall with hands.
3. Increase power on the shot as player (a) succeeds.
4. Player (b), vary the serve, speed, and angle, as player (a) shows improvement.

Role of Instructor

1. Watch for proper execution of the technique to ensure development and safety.
2. Make adjustments; first allow players the opportunity to experiment.
3. Switch and change the situation. For example, move player (a) further back, and alter the height of the serve.

Performance Benefits of Heading from the Knees

1. Allows a player to work at own pace.
2. Provides a successful environment for learning the technique.
3. Produces a safe situation to introduce the diving header.
4. Allows the instructor to monitor and change inappropriate methods by quickly pinpointing errors.
5. Excellent drill to lead into the full diving header from the standing position.

Drill Number Two

Diving Header from the Standing Position: Two serving players stand 3 to 5 yards apart facing the heading player. The heading player is stationed 10 to 15 yards away with the ball. The serving players alternate turns of tossing the ball. One server may toss a low ball while other may toss high balls. The focus is to adjust the positioning and moving to the various tosses. All players rotate until each has had an opportunity to serve the ball.

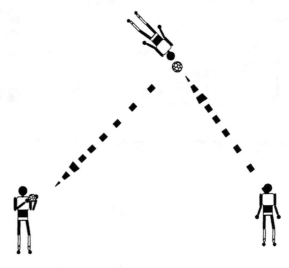

Fig. 3.20

Role of Player

1. Wait for pass.
2. Quickly stand after striking the ball.
3. Serve a nice lofted serve and increase the challenge after players have mastered the technique.

Role of Instructor

1. Focus on the execution of the technique, ensuring safety and proper skill.
2. Encourage the serving player to modify and create challenging serves by increasing the speed or altering the serving angle.
3. Change servers often.

Performance Benefits of Diving Header from the Standing Position

1. Pressure is limited while learning this technique.
2. Provides all players an opportunity for many repetitions.
3. Reinforces the technique in a realistic position, the standing position.

Drills to Develop Passing Techniques

Drill Number One

Volley Soccer: The players are divided into two groups of six or more. Movement is confined to either a circle or 20x20 foot grid area divided in the middle. The object of the drill is for one team to pass a ball across the mid-line and have it bounce twice before an opposing player can touch it. Play is initiated by a back player who kicks the ball over the mid-line and into the restricted playing of the opposite team. The team receiving the ball must pass in the air to three different teammates before sending the ball over the mid-line with the head. If the ball goes out-of-bounds, or consecutively touches the ground twice, the serving team receives one point. Points are only awarded on the serve. If a team does not score off their serve, the opposite team wins the serve and can attempt to score a point.

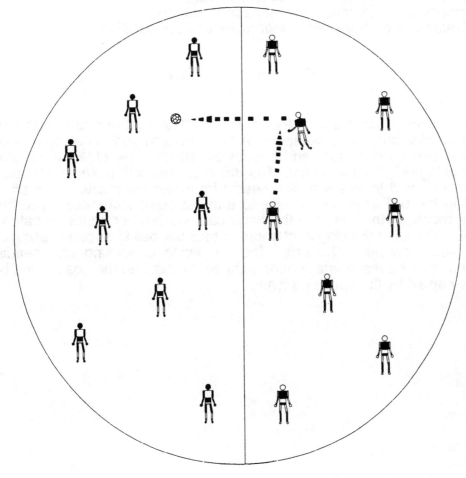

Fig. 3.21

Role of Player

1. Pass with a soft touch to teammates.
2. Search for open players to head across mid-line.
3. Make space for player controlling ball.
4. Don't forget to pass over mid-line with head.
5. Remember to pass three consecutive passes before sending ball over mid-line.

Role of Instructor

1. Reinforce quickness of feet and soft touches on ball.
2. Develop a rotation that places all players on front and back.
3. Focus the drill on the proper techniques of heading.

Performance Benefits of Volley Soccer

1. Develops ball control and coordination with all body parts.
2. Establishes a quick response to the ball.
3. Improves skill in heading to a specific location.
4. Creates an environment of teamwork and cooperation.

Drill Number Two

Toss and Head: This drill takes place in a 30x30 foot grid area with eight players a side and no goalkeepers. A modified size goal is placed on each sideline, two for one team and two for the other. The object is to score goals using only the head shot. The drill is started with a player who picks up the ball and tosses it to the head of another teammate. The player heading the ball attempts to pass to another open teammate. The third player receiving the ball from the head can use his/her hands to catch it. At this point, the third player attempts to toss the ball to another teammate who must now head the ball. The sequence of tossing and heading continues until a teammate is open to head the ball into the goal, or the ball is intercepted by the opposing team.

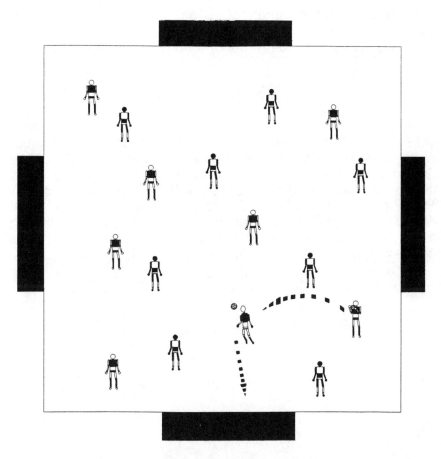

Fig. 3.22

Role of Player

1. Move to an open space to receive a pass.
2. Aggressively work forward to position a teammate for a head shot on goal.
3. Head to unmarked teammates.

Role of Instructor

1. Reinforce movement and penetration to the goals.
2. Encourage players to view a teammate or open space before initiating the head pass or shot.
3. Ensure players stay spread out, opening up passing and heading opportunities.

Performance Benefits of Toss and Head

1. Forces players to move and position themselves in open spaces.
2. Establishes the concept of finishing.

3. Creates a tactical environment of various movement patterns that lead to scoring chances.
4. Develops the skill of heading to a unmarked teammate.

Drill Number Three

Pass and Pursue: This drill is played with five players, three attackers and two defenders, in a 10x20 yard grid area. The grid is divided in half with three players on one side and two on the other. Players (a) and (b) are teammates who are attempting to pass the ball to player (c) positioned on the other side on the mid-line. The player who makes the pass to (c) moves across the mid-line and creates a two on one on the other side of the grid. The two defenders are attempting to block and steal the ball. The drill continues for a designed time frame then the players rotate.

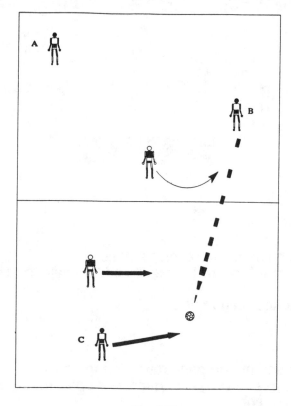

Fig. 3.23

Role of Player

1. Maintain a wide attacking position.
2. Move quickly after the pass to keep the defense off balance.
3. Pass with one and two touches on the ball.

Role of Instructor

1. Encourage quick movements after the pass.
2. Reinforce creativity and imagination in passing attempts.
3. Enforce one and two touch passing combinations when groups gain proficiency.

Performance Benefits of Pass and Pursue

1. Requires thinking in movement and passing.
2. Develops stamina.
3. Forces players to apply accurate and varied passes to teammates.

Drill Number Four

Modified Keep Away with a Free Zone: For this drill a grid area of 20x40 is developed with a 5 yard free zone in the middle. The drill utilizes four attackers and two defenders on each half (ten total players) on the grid. The object is to maintain ball possession. The attackers are first required to complete four consecutive passes. The fifth pass must be made to an attacker who moves into the free zone. Once that player has controlled the ball, he/she will pass the ball into the opposite side of the grid and creates a five on two situation. Again, attackers are to make four consecutive passes before another attacker can pass to a teammate in the free zone.

Fig. 3.24

Role of Player

1. Maintain possession by staying wide and creating open spaces for teammates.
2. Quickly move to an open space after each pass.
3. Observe the movement of defenders and counter by moving in the opposite direction.
4. Burst into the free zone after the fourth pass on a side.

Role of Instructor

1. Enforce one and two touch passing combinations.
2. Encourage quick and continuous movement.
3. Require appropriate spacing between players.

Performance Benefits of Modified Keep Away with a Free Zone

1. Develops passing combinations in challenging situations.
2. Creates a setting to improve in movement and field placement.
3. Improves skills in one and two touch passing.

Drill Number Five

Large Group Passing: This drill in played in a 20x40 grid with six players on a side. One modified goal (5 feet) is placed on each end-line with no goalkeepers. The object of the drill is to move the ball down field to score a goal. Passes are restricted to at least 8 to 10 yards. If a back pass is made, the next pass must be forward. The passing player must follow and support the ball carrier.

Fig. 3.25

Role of Player

1. Move and create open space.
2. Initiate deceptive feinting move.
3. Utilize all passing techniques to pass-to-the-feet of the open teammate.

Role of Instructor

1. Teach the proper timing of the movements.
2. Enforce the 8 to 10 yard passing rule.
3. Reinforce the proper positioning and execution of the pass.
4. Focus on the objective which is to score.

Performance Benefits of Large Group Passing

1. Creates a passing situation with scoring as a focus.
2. Institutes all the components (movement, control, proper passing, goal scoring) of a modified game setting.

Techniques in Trapping

Introduction

Trapping is a fundamental skill each player should possess. Balls move at different speeds, angles, heights, or with altering spins. A player needs to know how to manipulate select body parts to soften or cushion the impact thereby controlling the ball. The player who masters the various trapping techniques experience more time to either dribble, pass to another teammate, or shoot on goal.

Trapping is a skill that requires athletic ability and composure. During game situations, a player is often confronted with an unexpected pass or rebound. Responding to these situations with the appropriate technique will help the ball handler maintain possession. If the pace or spin of the ball is misjudged, it ends up bouncing off the foot or chest to the opposing team. Knowledge of appropriate techniques, concentration, and proper execution of trapping skill are essential elements of any foundation in a team's attack.

When trapping, it is desired to have the ball stop at the feet if one is in a stationary position. If the player is on the run, it is recommended that the ball land slightly ahead of the body (possibly two to three yards, depending on the location of the opponents). The closer one keeps the ball to the body, the more likely a player will maintain possession.

This chapter will introduce four basic trapping techniques. Each method is introduced with teaching points followed by common faults and corrections. Drills are incorporated to develop each trapping method. The role of the player and instructor will be presented with performance benefits of each drill.

Trapping with the Inside-of-the-Foot

Similar to passing with the inside-of-the-foot, the inside-of-the-foot trap is the most commonly used trapping technique. Players who begin to master this type of trap will witness immediate benefits from consistent ball control.

Teaching Points for Trapping with the Inside–of–the–Foot

1. Move in the direction of approaching ball.
2. Non-trapping foot should point in the direction of the approaching ball.
3. The leg of the non-trapping foot should be slightly bent.
4. The foot should be turned 90 degrees to create a large surface area for trapping.
5. Shoulder should be square and face the on coming ball.
6. The trapping foot should be held off the ground and positioned slightly ahead of the body.
7. Eyes are on the ball.
8. Trunk leans back slightly.
9. Ankle of trapping foot is rigid.
10. As ball makes contact the side of foot, draw foot back to cushion ball and soften the impact.
11. The foot should contact the center or top portion of the ball.
12. Ball should stop just in front of body.
13. More cushion might be needed on certain passes, it depends on the pace of the ball. For balls approaching at faster speeds, place the trapping foot farther in front of the body and allow more give with the trapping foot.

Photo 4.1 - 4.2

Common Faults and Corrections

Fault

Ball bounces off trapping foot and away from body.

Correction

1. Leg of trapping foot is too rigid, cushion the blow by moving lower leg back during ball contact.
2. Ball contacts heal of foot while foot is on the ground, place foot in the air and contact with the center portion of the inside of the foot.
3. Foot strikes a ball while foot is turned up and the sole of the foot is exposed to ball.

Fault

Ball bounces over foot.

Correction

1. Move the foot off the ground.
2. Ball contact should be on the center or upper portion of ball.

Fault

Ball bounces up in the air.

Correction

1. Foot contact on the ball should be on the center or upper portion of the ball.
2. Foot needs to be off the ground.

Trapping with the Outside–of–the–Foot

Frequently, players receive a quick and unexpected pass that requires ball control with the outside-of-the-foot. During game situations players may receive a ball in a tight congested situation (possibly the penalty box) which requires swift movement, control, and a quick release of the ball. To do this successfully, players use the outside-of-the-foot to trap.

Teaching Points for Trapping with the Outside–of–the–Foot

1. Weight of body placed on non-trapping foot.
2. Leg and foot of receiving ball drawn back.
3. Body leans in the direction of approaching ball.
4. Eyes on ball; head down.
5. Angle of trapping foot is rigid.
6. Trapping foot should be off the ground.

7. Outside of the foot, just below the top of the instep, makes contact on the center or top portion of the ball.
8. During ball contact with outside of foot, lower leg is drawn in to cushion ball.
9. Ball should stop in front of the body after controlling it and head is up viewing the field for options of passing, shooting, or dribbling.

Photo 4.3

Common Faults and Corrections

Fault

Ball bounces off foot too far in front of body.

Correction

1. Receiving leg too stiff.
2. Foot of receiving leg needs to be off the ground.
3. Retract receiving leg to cushion the ball, adjust depending on speed of approaching ball.

Fault

Ball bounces over trapping foot.

Correction

1. Trapping foot needs to be off the ground.
2. Contact the center portion of the ball.

Drills to Develop Trapping with the Inside and Outside–of–the–Foot

Each drill is listed in order of difficulty. As the player begins to master this technique, instructors are encouraged to make the practice more challenging. This can be accomplished by increasing the speed, movement, or pressure on the person trapping the ball.

Drill Number One

Passing to Partner: During this drill partners are to pass the ball to a teammate. The receiving partner will trap with either the inside or outside-of-the-foot. It should be reinforced to players that moving toward the pass will prevent the opposition from moving in front and stealing the ball away. After passing the ball, the player should back up 3 to 5 yards and prepare to move forward for the next pass.

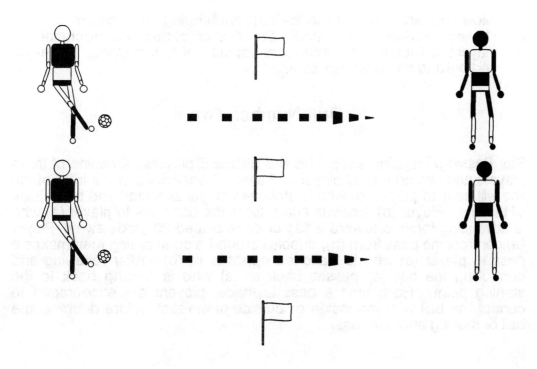

Fig. 4.1

Role of Player

1. Move in the direction of the ball before trapping it.
2. Pass a ball on the ground to ensure success of trapping partner.
3. Make personal adjustments depending on what occurs with the ball.
4. Increase the pace of the pass as partner becomes successful with the appropriate trapping technique.
5. Alter the direction of the pass to increase adjustment abilities to various situations and angles.

Role of Instructor

1. Have the partners start out passing the ball at a slow pace, then increase the speed as partners become proficient.
2. Partners should begin at a stationary position first, as they gain skill have them move in the direction of the pass.
3. Encourage a quick release with consistent control.
4. Watch for innappropriate techniques and common faults. Make adjustments when necessary.

Performance Benefits of Passing to Partner

1. Allows players to practice in the least challenging environment.
2. Players can develop and modify the situation at their own discretion.
3. Players will learn the mechanical aspects of this trapping technique and build to an advanced level.

Drill Number Two

Star Passing/Trapping Drill: This drill utilizes 5 players. One line of three players and two additional players. Player (a) positioned in the front of the line will pass to player (b) who is stationed 10 yards ahead and to the side of the line. Player (b) receives and returns the ball back to player (a) who is advancing forward toward a flag or cone placed 20 yards away. Player (a) controls the pass from (b), dribbles around a cone or flag then makes a pass to player (c) who is stationed opposite of (b). After receiving and controlling the ball (c) passes back to (a) who is moving back to the starting point. Each time a pass is made, players are encouraged to control the ball with the inside or outside-of-the-foot before dribbling the ball or making another pass.

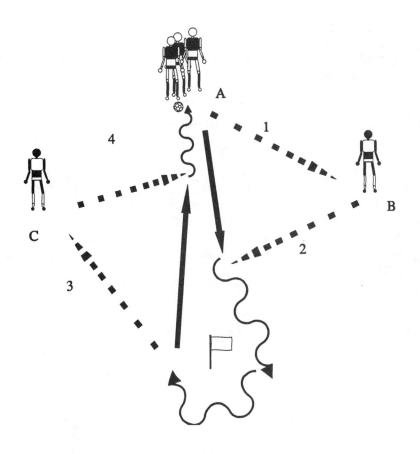

Fig. 4.2

Role of Player

1. Quickly gain control of the ball before returning a pass.
2. Make passes on the ground to help ensure proper trapping of the inside of the foot.
3. Keep eyes on the ball and playing area while advancing through drill.

Role of Instructor

1. Encourage players to advance though the drill as quickly as possible.
2. Switch outside players, (b) and (c), often.
3. Focus in on common faults, balls bouncing too far in front of players. Make appropriate adjustments.
4. Encourage players to trap with both feet.
5. Change the direction of the drill by making player (a) pass first to (c).

Performance Benefits of Star Passing/Trapping Drill

1. Players are forced to trap the ball while on the move.
2. Players will trap with both feet.

3. Players can adjust the speed and pace of the drill on their own depending on individual performance.
4. Players must successfully respond to balls approaching from different angles and speeds.

Drill Number Three

Trapping and Moving: In a 10x10 foot grid area three players are placed in the center with one ball. When instructed to start, players are asked to move around and pass the ball after each trap. Continual movement is encouraged, each player in the grid area should be active. Limit players to two touches, one for the trap and the second for the pass. Focus on trapping with both the inside and outside-of-the-feet. Creativity should be a secondary focus.

Fig. 4.3

Role of Player

1. Move in the direction of the pass.
2. Quickly control and release the next pass.
3. Keep eyes on partners and ball when receiving and passing.
4. Movement in the grid area should be continuous for each player.

Role of Instructor

1. Encourage continuous movement.
2. Reinforce the two touch rule.
3. Encourage creativity and improvision.

Performance Benefits of Trapping and Moving

1. To encourage development in trapping a ball while moving.
2. To force a player to analyze various passing angles and adjust to them.
3. To develop trapping skills while under pressure.
4. To force a quick control and quick release of the ball.

Trapping the Volley

It is not uncommon for a player to receive a bouncing ball. When this occurs, the player must apply the volley trap. This will help soften the force created by the ball and bring it back under control. When a bouncing ball is approaching, position the body in its path and bring a foot up to its height. The ball should contact the inside-of-the-foot. Once under control, the player is in position to move forward.

Teaching Points for The Volley Trap

1. Body should be positioned in line with balls path.
2. Point toe of non-trapping foot in path of ball.
3. Turn knee out to create a flat surface area with inside-of-the-foot.
4. Body should be upright with a loose trapping leg.
5. Receive ball with inside-of-the-foot.
6. During contact, cushion ball by drawing foot back behind body.
7. Allow ball to fall to the ground.

Common Faults and Corrections

Fault

Ball bounces off foot several feet in front of player.

Correction

1. Foot it too rigid, ankle should be slightly loose.
2. Draw leg back during contact.

Fault

Ball goes under or over foot.

Correction

Eye height of ball and adjust to ground surfaces.

Trapping with the Thigh

Often, players are confronted with balls approaching near the base of the hip at their mid-line. The most effective body part used to control this type of ball is the thigh. The principles for trapping with the thigh are the same as with the inside-of-the-foot. The thigh should be raised up to receive the ball, then at the point of contact drawn back to cushion the force of the ball.

Teaching Points for Trapping with the Thigh

1. Body should face the approaching ball and be positioned under its flight.
2. Shoulders square.
3. Non-kicking foot facing the path of ball.
4. Knee of non-kicking foot slightly bent.
5. Head should be down with eyes on the ball.
6. Upper trunk should lean slightly forward.
7. Trapping thigh should be raised parallel to the ground to receive the ball.
8. During ball contact, thigh should be retracted back to cushion the impact.
9. Ball should drop in front of the body.

Photos 4.4 - 4.5

Common Faults and Corrections

Fault

Ball bounces off thigh and away from player.

Correction

1.   Retract thigh to cushion force of impact.

2. Ball should contact the center portion of thigh.
3. Thigh is rising during ball contact, make sure the thigh cushions the ball by withdrawing the ball at the moment of contact.

Drills to Develop Skills of Trapping with the Thigh

Each drill in this series allows the player numerous repetitions for thigh trapping. Instructors are encouraged to interject all passing and trapping techniques while practicing the proper method of thigh trapping. Instructors are reminded to seek about 80 percent proficiency before moving on, especially when players are just beginning to understand the mechanics of this trap.

Drill Number One

Partner Serving: During this drill one player will serve a lofted ball to his/her partner who traps it with either the right or left thigh, then passes it back with a specified method. The serving partner should continue to serve several times before switching with the trapping partner.

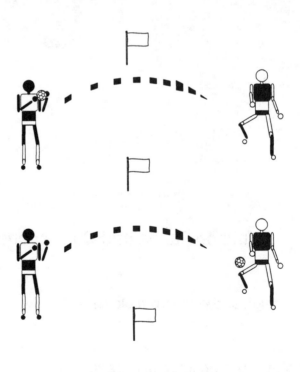

Fig. 4.4

Role of Player

1. Serve a soft lofted ball which allows the trapping partner sufficient time to position himself/herself underneath it and make a successful trap.
2. Trap with both thighs.
3. The server should alter the direction and height of the ball as proficiency is gained.

Role of Instructor

1. Encourage players to serve an easy lofted ball when paired with an inexperienced player. This will allow sufficient time to comprehend the technique.
2. As players become proficient, reinforce challenging serves by increasing the distance between partners and/or having the server loft a ball from various angles and heights.

Performance Benefits of Partner Passing

1. Players work at own pace.
2. It creates a situation where players can master the trapping method with limited challenge or pressure.

Drill Number Two

Trapping a Chipped Ball: This drill involves three players positioned in a line and separated by ten to fifteen yards. Player (a) passes a ball on the ground to player (c) who chips the ball to player (b) who is stationed between the other two. Player (b) attempts to trap the ball by using the thigh trap. After the trap (b) passes the ball back to (a).

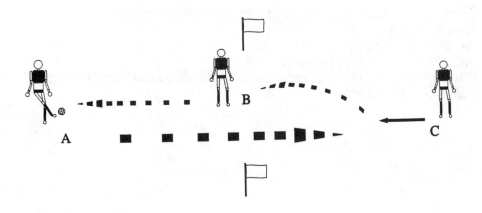

Fig. 4.5

Role of Player

1. Ensure proper passing & trapping techniques.
2. Emphasis is on the two-touch, except for the middle player (b) whose focus is either two or three touch.

Role of Instructor

1. Watch for innapporpriate execution and common faults in each technical aspect of the drill. Make adjustments when necessary.
2. Adjust the distances separating the players depending on the success of the group.

Performance Benefits of Trapping a Chipped Ball

1. Players are forced to trap with the thigh off a chipped ball.
2. Players incorporate various passing techniques which culminate into a trap with the thigh.

Trapping with the Chest

Balls which approach a player at the chest or head will require a chest trap. Those with limited confidence and insufficient technical ability in the chest trap often lose ball possession. This results in missed opportunities that could lead to scoring. Instructors need to provide each player with sufficient time to master this trapping technique, a method often overlooked.

Teaching Points for Trapping with the Chest

1. Body should face approaching ball, shoulders square.
2. Knees slightly bent.
3. Head steady with eyes on the ball.
4. Arch body back to receive the ball.
5. During ball contact, chest should withdrawal to cushion the impact.
6. Ball drops at the feet.

Photos 4.6 - 4.8

Common Faults and Corrections

Fault

Ball bounces away from chest.

Correction

1. Bend at waist, allow enough give to cushion the ball.
2. Body might be too rigid; bend knees and withdrawal with force of impact.

Fault

Ball bounces too high after making contact with the chest.

Correction

*   Avoid arching the upper truck. Refrain from leaning back too far.

Drills to Develop Skills of Trapping with the Chest

Drills to develop this trapping technique are similar to other traps. The key is found by cushioning the ball at the point of impact. The sequence and progression to master this technique needs to be slow. As players progress through the drills, instructors can reinforce all passing and trapping skills previously learned.

It is recommended that instructors continue to work and develop each passing and trapping method throughout the year. As instructors introduce more challenging situations to players, the proficiency and consistency will escalate.

Drill Number One

Partner Passing: The chest pass is best introduced to players when a partner serves the ball with a controlled lofted pass to the partners chest. (See Drill Number One For Thigh Trapping)

Drill Number Two

Man in the Middle: (See Drill Number Three in Passing with the Inside-of-the-Foot). During this drill players toss a high lofted ball to the man in the middle who is to chest trap, then pass the ball back with either the inside, outside, or instep pass. As the man in the middle gains proficiency, outside players are encouraged to toss balls of various heights, angles, and speeds to further lead the middle player to mastery. All trapping and passing skills can be used during this drill.

Drill Number Three

Trapping a Chipped Ball: (See Drill Number Two in Thigh Trapping) During this drill, players use the thigh and chest trap depending on the height of the approaching ball.

Shooting Skills

Introduction

The purpose of mastering all the essential elements of attack is to place a player in a shooting position. Once this has been achieved, the player must have the conviction (willingness) to shoot. Many players possess the technical abilities of shooting by don't carry the proper attitude. If a player does not possess this attitude he/she will have a tendency to pass the responsibility to someone else. This unfortunate action results in missed opportunities and fewer goals. When given the opportunity to shoot, shoot!

It is also important for each player to learn and master the various shooting methods described in this chapter. Drills designed to develop shooting should be altered or modified to meet the individual needs of the players representing various skill levels. Instructors are encouraged to produce training sessions that allow players to execute each shooting technique from several distances and angles. Generating experiences that resemble "game like" situations (modified soccer games and/or experiences) will prepare players for a traditional game setting. Instructors are encouraged to create shooting drills that begin by introducing the player to the appropriate method, then increase the challenge by adding one or two defenders. This added pressure will help refine and develop the proper technique.

Five fundamental rules need to be remembered when shooting. They include:

1. Rule One: (**Proper Attitude and Movement**) Turn quickly and face the goal, shoot early, and shoot around an opponent.
2. Rule Two: (**Proper Distance**) First, power shots are usually outside the penalty area. Second, controlled shots generally occur when positioned closer to goal.
3. Rule Three: (**Accuracy**) Never sacrifice accuracy for power.
4. Rule Four: (**Shoot Low**) Shots of low trajectory are more advantageous than high shots. A team can benefit from a deflection or rebound off a defender or teammate.
5. Rule Five: (**Mental Aspects**) Confidence and composure are essential when the shooter is clear of defenders. Believe your shot is on target and will score.

Depending on the situation, each drill needs to incorporate each rule. Yet, modifications will be a factor in the learning process. This shooting section will involve the instep drive, volley, and side volley.

Shooting with the Instep

The shooting method of choice used 15 yards or more from the goal is the instep or instep drive. This technique yields an accurate and powerful shot. Players should use the instep drive while maintaining a focus of accuracy, not power. Once the procedure is mastered, players can impart more power on the ball.

Teaching Points for Shooting With the Instep

1. Approach the ball straight on.
2. Glance at the target just before contact.
3. When moving forward, the last stride before contact should be lengthened. (This allows a greater range of motion for the kicking leg).
4. Head and shoulders are projected forward.
5. Eyes on the ball.
6. The knee of the non-kicking leg should be slightly bent.
7. The non-kicking foot should be pointed to the target and placed along side the ball during contact.
8. The arm opposite the kicking leg should be pulled slightly across the body.
9. The toe of the kicking leg should be pointed down creating a flat surface for the instep to strike the ball.
10. Contact the center portion of the ball with the top of the instep.
11. The ankle must be rigid to ensure a solid contact on the ball.
12. The kicking leg, after ball contact, should extend toward the target.

Photos 5.1 - 5.2

Common Faults and Corrections

Fault

Ball lacks accuracy.

Correction

1. Contact the midline of the ball.
2. Strike the ball straight on, don't lean away from it.
3. Move arm opposite the kicking leg forward and slightly in front of the body.
4. Toe of non-kicking foot must point in the direction of target.
5. Head should be down and steady with eyes on the ball.

Fault

Ball lacks sufficient power.

Correction

1. Ankle of kicking leg must be rigid.
2. Contact the middle portion of the ball; foot may be hitting too high on the ball forcing it into the ground.
3. The stride before ball contact must be lengthen, this will allow a greater range on motion resulting in a more powerful shot.

Fault

Ball rises into the air.

Correction

1. Strike the center portion of the ball.
2. Keep your head down and steady.
3. Make contact on the ball when it is next to the non-kicking foot.
4. Ankle of kicking foot should be rigid with toe pointing down.

Drills to Develop Shooting with the Instep

Drills should reflect shots from several angles and speeds. In game situations, a player will confront various challenges and conditional changes. Successful players adapt and execute the most effective shooting technique dictated by each situation. During practice sessions, instructors create various settings to prepare individuals to successfully respond and adapt to these changing circumstances. The drills listed below can be used and modified to meet the needs of certain groups instructors are responsible for training.

Drill Number One

Shooting a Ball Coming from Various Directions: During this drill two players are paired, one serving and one shooting. The shooting player is positioned approximately 18 to 20 yards from goal. Upon a signal the serving player will pass the ball from various angles and speeds to the shooting player who is attempting to place a shot into the corners of the goal. The angle of the serve will vary: (1) rolling toward the shooter, (2) rolling away from the shooter, and (3) rolling toward the shooter from the right and left sides.

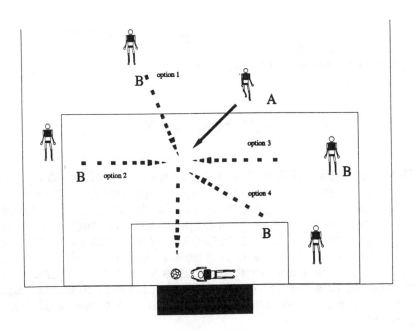

Fig. 5.1

Role of Player

1. Be patient when moving into position to execute the proper shooting technique.
2. Quickly glance at target before turning eyes back to the ball when shooting.
3. Servers are encouraged to pass the ball at various speeds to force the shooter to make necessary adjustments while properly shooting with the instep.
4. Server should pass a ball into the designated position.

Role of Instructor

1. Rotate the shooter and server as the shooting player becomes successful.
2. Emphasize the proper technique and make adjustments when needed.
3. Optional drill formation:

   Have four or five players positioned in various areas to provide the shooter with
   different angles to shoot from during each individual session.

Performance Benefits of Shooting a Ball Coming from Various Directions

1. Players are receiving passes from several angles and speeds while executing the instep drive.

2. Players are practicing the technique under limited pressure to allow for proper skill acquisition.
3. Players can advance at own pace.

Drill Number Two

Quick Release: During this drill 5 to 6 players are positioned outside a 25 to 30 yard circle. Three corner flags or poles are positioned in the center of the circle about 6 yards apart in triangular formation (this creates three goals to shoot on). Two goalkeepers are placed inside the circle defending the three goals. The outside players pass between themselves attempting to open up a section of a goal to shoot on. If players are given an open shot, they are encouraged to take it. If not, they should pass it to a player in better position to shoot. Outside players are encouraged to one or two-touch all passes or shots to keep the goalkeepers off balance and out of position.

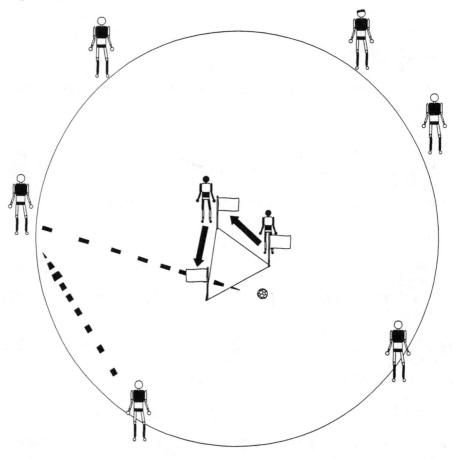

Fig. 5.2

Role of Player

1. Quickly release the ball and eye the position of the goalkeeper before shooting.
2. Move the ball around the circle to get the goalkeepers out of position.
3. Keep shots low.
4. When given the opportunity to shoot then shoot, don't pass up the responsibility.

Role of Instructor

1. Encourage proper execution of the instep drive, make adjustments when shooting errors occur.
2. Add a second ball to increase the timing, reactions, and ball contact opportunities.

Performance Benefits of Quick Release

1. Allows a player the opportunity to shoot off a quick pass.
2. Forces a player to select the spot on the goal when shooting.
3. Requires a player to choose either to shoot or pass, depending on the situation and position of the goalkeeper.

Drill Number Three

Shooting from a Wall Pass: This drill involves four players, a shooter, passer, defender, and goalkeeper. The shooter, player (a) positioned 25 to 30 yards from goal, passes the ball to player (b) then moves forwards toward the goal. Player (b) will one-touch the ball back to (a). At this point, the defender, player (c), will move off the end-line and attempt to defend the goal. The shooter (a) will execute the instep drive, attempting to beat the goalkeeper.

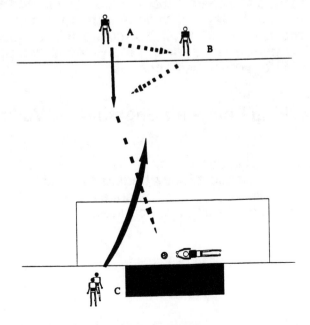

Role of Player

1. Shooter needs to glance at the goal before shooting attempt.
2. Passing player (b) needs to pass a slow and controlled ball on the ground to the shooting player.
3. Defender is reminded to not leave the end-line until first pass is completed.

Role of Instructor

1. Monitor the movements and distances, make adjustments when needed.
2. Adjust the defensive position depending on the success and performance of the shooter, he/she should be successful first. Encourage the shooter to glance up at a selected spot in the goal just before shooting.
4. Modify the situation by asking the server to alter a pass to either the right or the left side of the body.

Performance Benefits of Shooting from a Wall Pass

1. Provides pressure on the shooting player.
2. Forces the shooter to beat a goalkeeper in a full size goal with an approaching defender.
3. Requires the shooting player to adjust to the various passing angles from (b).

Shooting the Volley

When attacking the opposing goal, players often confront balls in flight. The shooting technique utilized in these situations is the "volley." Since the ball is traveling in the air it allows the shooter to initiate a complete and uninhibited leg swing. This allows the ball to be more responsive after contact. A player tends to generate tremendous power and velocity on the ball when shooting the volley. It is important to remind a player that patience and timing are critical when executing this shooting technique. When appropriately performed, shooting the volley allows opportunities to score exciting goals from great distances.

Teaching Points for Shooting the Volley

1. Body square with ball in approach.
2. Non-kicking foot is placed slightly behind ball with toe pointed in the direction of target, knee is bent for balance.
3. Head is down and steady with eyes on the ball.

4. Arm opposite kicking leg is brought across body with shoulder pointed in the direction of the target.
5. Upper trunk leans forward.
6. Kicking leg is drawn back and bent at the knee.
7. Ankle of kicking leg is maximally extended in the plantar flexed position with toe pointing down.
8. Contact should occur when the ball is positioned slightly in front of the non-kicking leg.
9. Snap the leg forward and strike the center or middle portion of the ball.
10. Ankle of kicking leg is rigid with toe pointing down.
11. The kicking leg will continue forward in the direction of the target with a complete follow through.

Photos 5.3. - 5.4

Common Faults and Corrections

Fault

Ball travels extremely high into the air.

Correction

1. Body is leaning back, it should be leaning forward over ball during contact.
2. Instep strikes ball too early. Ensure the ball is slightly ahead of the non-kicking foot before making contact, be patient and wait for the appropriate time.
3. Head and eyes might be looking up, make sure eyes are on the ball while head is down and steady.

4. Instep is making contact with the lower section of the ball. Make sure you contact the center or top portion.

Fault

Ball lacks accuracy.

Correction

1. Arm opposite kicking foot should be brought forward and slightly across the body.
2. Non-kicking foot should be pointing toward target.
3. Eyes should be on the ball.
4. Leg is snapped forward into the ball.
5. Leg movement should continue in the direction of the target.

Fault

Ball lacks sufficient power and velocity.

Correction

1. Ankle of kicking leg should remain rigid.
2. Kicking leg is snapped forward with complete follow through in the direction of the target.

Drills to Develop Shooting the Volley

A major emphasis when shooting the volley is timing and patience. Players often rush the shot and move the kicking leg prematurely through the movement. Drills should be designed to promote patience to accurately time the kick in relation to the pace, height, and direction of the ball.

Drill Number One

Partner Serving Partner Shooting on Goal: During this drill two shooters are matched with two servers and two goals (with or without goalkeepers). Shooter (a), positioned 20 to 25 yards from goal, receives a lofted pass from a server (1) who is positioned at the post of the goal. The shooter moves toward the serve, allowing one or two bounces before contact. After player (a) shoots the volley, player (b) receives a lofted pass from a server (2). This person is positioned on the goal post opposite server (1). As shooters become proficient, modify the drill by having the shooters strike a ball moving away from them. Have the server positioned behind the shooter, serve a lofted ball from the back. Now the shooting player must adjust his/her approach by reacting to a new situation. The drill can be further modified by having the two serving players move about 8 yards inside the corners of the penalty box where the penalty line meets the end-line. From this position, servers are asked to chip a ball to the top of the penalty box, about 18 yards from goal. Shooters move and adjust depending on the angle, pace, and movement of the approaching ball. Instructors are encouraged to place goalkeepers into the goal during one of the modifications.

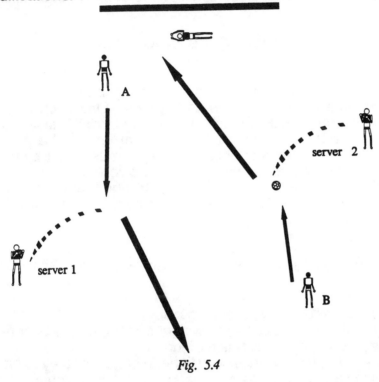

Fig. 5.4

Role of Player

1. Make a decision on where movement should be before setting up to shoot
2. Be patient before reacting to the ball.
3. Make adjustments based from teaching points above.
4. Server should loft a soft high ball to the shooter.
5. If the situation allows it, it is easier to strike a ball that is falling compared to rising. Wait for the ball to drop then execute the shot.

Role of Instructor

1. Re-position and modify the servers location depending on the success of the shooting player.
2. Monitor all sessions and make adjustments based off shooting outcomes.

3. Switch shooters and servers when appropriate.
4. Section off specific shooting areas of the goal.

Performance Benefits of Partner Serving Partner Shooting on Goal

1. Allows players to make personal adjustments while providing several repetitions and opportunities to master the technique.
2. As the instructor or teacher modifies the drill, players are forced to execute under more and more challenging situations.
3. Players are able to make adjustments based from visual results.

Shooting the Side–Volley

During game situations players in scoring position are faced with approaching balls from all heights and angles. One such challenge that consistently confronts attackers is balls coming from the side. Often times these balls are passed in the air from the corners of the field, like in a crossing situation. When this occurs, a player must react by trapping the ball or shooting with either the head or the side volley.

The side volley is a difficult technique but one that is essential. When implementing the side volley, a player is reminded to shoot with the foot nearest the ball.

Teaching Points for Shooting with the Side Volley

1. Body should face the approaching ball.
2. The leg of the non-kicking foot (weight bearing leg) is bent at the knee with toe pointing in the direction of the target.
3. Arms are extended for balance with head steady and eyes on the ball.
4. The kicking leg is raised to the side, parallel to the ground.
5. Ankle of the kicking leg draws the foot back in the extended position.
6. Lean body slightly back to compensate for leg action.
7. Rotate the body on the balanced foot.
8. Snap the kicking leg toward and through the top half of the ball, contacting the ball with the instep and moving the leg in a downward motion.
9. Complete the rotation during contact and into the follow through.
10. Kicking leg drops to the ground after contact.
11. Keep eyes on the ball.

Photos 5.5 - 5.6

Common Faults and Corrections

Fault

Ball rises into the air over the target.

Correction

1. Contact the center or top portion of the ball.
2. During the kicking motion, the leg should swing slightly down toward the ground.

Fault

Ball lacks accuracy.

Correction

1. Eyes on ball.
2. Lean slightly back to compensate for appropriate leg swing.
3. Ankle is rigid with toe pointing down during contact.

Fault

Ball lacks power and velocity.

Correction

1. Ankle and leg is too stiff.
2. Leg swing initiates a snapping action just before ball contact.
3. Complete the kicking action with a thorough follow through.

Drills to Develop Shooting the Side Volley

This technique is one of the most difficult to master for any age group. The biomechanical components are a culmination of several other passing/shooting methods. Instructors are encouraged to have the player develop and master all other passing/shooting challenges before attempting to introduce this specific technique.

Drills designed to develop this method are similar to the volley, with one minor exception. The placement of the server is to the side of the shooter. When teaching this shooting style, introduce and demonstrate the basic components by breaking down the inter-related parts. Patience and multiple repetitions are essential to perfecting the side volley.

Drill Number One

Partner Serving Partner Shooting: During this drill one server and one shooter are matched together. The shooter is positioned 8 to 10 yards from a goal, fence, or wall. The server, positioned 5 to 10 yards from the shooter lofts a ball at a 35 degree angle to the shooter. The shooter should allow the ball to bounce once, allowing time to make any bodily adjustments before attempting the shot. Players are asked to shoot and serve several times before rotating.

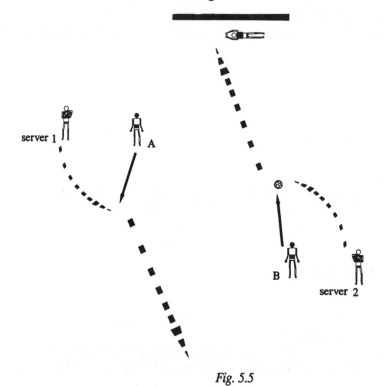

Fig. 5.5

Role of Player

1. Patiently wait for the ball. Don't rush the execution of the technique.
2. The server can provide feedback on the delivery and performance of the shot to the shooter.
3. Server needs to adjust the toss until the appropriate angle is discovered.
4. As shooter gains proficiency, the server can move back or change the angle of the serve.

Role of Instructor

1. Rotate server and shooter depending on success and consistency of the shot.
2. Focus in on the technique and make appropriate adjustments when needed.
3. If the player is unsuccessful, demonstrate once again with one of the players who is successful. This will reinforce the proper method.

Performance Benefits of Partner Serving Partner Shooting on Goal

1. Allow players numerous repetitions.
2. Pressure during the session is limited.
3. Allows a player to progress and modify at a controlled pace.

Drill Number Two

Partner Serving Partner Shooting on Goal (Modification): This drill is the same as drill number one in Shooting the Volley, but with on minor modification, the placement of the server. During this drill, the server should be placed parallel to the shooter about 20 to 25 yards away. The server then chips the ball toward the shooter. (See Figure From Drill Number One in Shooting the Volley).

Drills to Develop Shooting Skills

Drill Number One

Shooting From Outside the Fifteen: Create a grid area of 20x30 with goals and goalkeepers placed on the end-line. The gird is divided in half with three players positioned on each side. The object is for the attackers (a & b) to pass to the striker (c) who is attempting to get away from the two defenders and into position to shoot. If a scoring opportunity does not materialize for the striker, a back pass to either teammate may produce a scoring chance. Players are restricted to their side of the field. Once a goal is scored or the ball kicked out-of-bounds, the situation changes with the defenders becoming attackers and attackers becoming defenders.

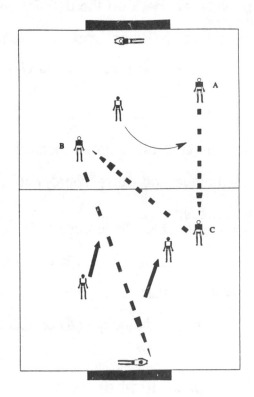

Fig. 5.6

Role of Player

1. Don't hold the ball long, keep moving it around the field.
2. Freely shoot past the 15 yard mark if feasible.
3. Initiate feinting moves to force the defender off balance.

Role of Instructor

1. Maintain the focus of shooting.
2. Rotate the striker often.
3. Encourage continuous movement with all players.

Performance Benefits to Shooting from Outside the Fifteen

1. Forces a striker to fight for a open position to shoot.
2. Improves performance in support and penetrating runs.
3. Develops cardiovascular fitness while perfecting shooting skills in a game related situation.

Drill Number Two

Six on Six Shooting Drill: Twelve players are placed in a 30x50 yard grid area with one goal with goalkeeper positioned on each end-line. The exercise is a modified game situation with a two-touch passing restriction and an emphasis of first time shooting.

Fig. 5.7

Role of Player

1. Always look for the open shot.
2. Shoot first time, don't wait.
3. Emphasis one and two-touch passing.

Role of Instructor

1. Reinforce the proper attitude and shooting conviction.
2. Encourage a quick release of the ball.
3. Keep the drill going by having a generous supply of balls.

Performance Benefits of Six on Six Shooting Drill

1. Instills an attack mentality.
2. Develops shooting skills from all angles and distances.
3. Refines shooting in a game related situation.
4. Improves skill and knowledge in proper positioning, a quick-release, and successful ball control.

Dribbling

Introduction

Dribbling is one of the most exciting and creative components of soccer. A player who can move with the ball past opponents with flair and imagination has spent countless hours practicing ball handling moves and feinting skills. Deception and disguise are key factors in dribbling the ball. Players who can mask their intentions and place opponents off balance are dangerous to opposing teams.

Two major categories of dribbling exist. The first includes moving with a ball close to your feet. The second involves moving the ball ahead of you about 3 to 5 yards by pushing it forward while you are running down field. The purpose of the first dribbling style is to maintain possession and ball control while confronting opposing players in tight spaces. The second type is used for pushing the ball quickly down an open field.

Dribbling the Ball Close to Feet

Dribbling the ball and keeping it close to the feet is a critical skill for each player on the field to learn. The player entering the attacking area of the field is often confronted with tightly packed and crowded penalty areas. A player who has the ability to challenge opponents with his/her dribbling skills create scoring opportunities. Traits associated with successful dribbling include disguise, deception, feinting techniques, and quick changes of direction.

Teaching Points for Dribbling a Ball Close to the Feet

1. Ball contacts a portion of foot.
2. Knees flexed with body in crouched position.
3. Head up, eyes scanning field, foot touching ball to provide feedback on its location.
4. Glance at ball when moving forward.
5. Body initiates feinting moves to get opposing player off balance.
6. Push ball with either the outside or inside portion of the foot in the opposite direction of the opponent.
7. If necessary, change the speed and direction to get defender off balance.

8. Keep your foot as close to the ball as possible during the entire maneuver (no more than one foot away).
9. After the defender is beat, quickly look up to see opportunities ahead.

Photos 6.1 - 6.2

Common Faults and Corrections of Faults

Fault

Player loses control of ball.

Correction

1. Contact ball with light soft touches.
2. Keep the ball as close and under the body as much as possible.
3. Don't impart too much force onto the ball.

Fault

Player loses awareness of balls location.

Correction

1. Instructors need to develop drills that create ball awareness skills.
2. The player might get distracted and lose concentration.
3. Practice for a certain level of confidence and control.

Drills for Developing Dribbling Techniques

Successful dribbling during game situations requires skill, talent, confidence, and control. Developing these traits demands practice sessions with limited pressure and challenge. This allows the player to be successful before advancing to competitive situations. As a player becomes comfortable while moving and controlling the ball with both feet, instructors can create situations with increased pressure to further challenge the player and refine his/her skill.

This section will introduce the reader to activities that develop a foundation in dribbling methods. Once players are comfortable with the ball, instructors can teach specific dribbling moves listed in this chapter. The chapter concludes with dribbling drills that utilize specific moves and feinting skills during competitive situations.

Drills to Develop Ball Awareness

Drill Number One

Becoming Acquainted with the Ball: Each player should be positioned with a ball inside a 30 X 30 foot grid area. On the command, the player is to move the ball around the grid, pushing the ball with the inside and outside of both feet while attempting to keep the head up. The player is encouraged to not touch one another or the ball of others. Creative actions including starting and stopping, quick changes of direction, and so on, are emphasized while players maintain ball control.

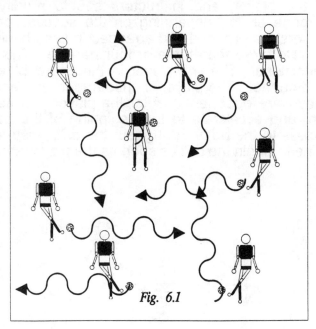

Fig. 6.1

Role of Player

1. Continue movements for designate time.
2. Be creative as possible. Move around an imaginary opponent.
3. Keep the head up and view surroundings.
4. Use both feet.

Role of Instructor

1. Stay on the outside of the grid to view all players.
2. Verbally reinforce desired movements, changes in direction, utilization of both feet, and starting and stopping actions.
3. Modify the activity by having a player switch with a partner after the instructor stops the action. This will reinforce the concept of keeping the head up while attempting to eye another player while dribbling.

Performance Benefits of Becoming Acquainted with the Ball

1. A player becomes comfortable with the ball.
2. Encourages development of both feet.
3. Develops creativity.
4. Reinforces the concept of keeping the head up.
5. Each player is active 100 percent of the time.

Drill Number Two

Dribbling Through Markers: 5 to 10 cones or flags are arranged in a straight line about three to four feet apart (this depends on the experience and ability of the player, and instructors should modify the distance between each cone or flag depending on the success or failure of the individual). Players are grouped and arranged in lines behind the rows of cones or flags. No more than three or four per line. This ensures large amounts of repetitions. The first player in the line dribbles through the markers using both feet. The player is encouraged to react to each cone or flag as if they were opponents. After the player passes all obstacles, they are to turn and accelerate to the beginning of the line. Attempt to keep the ball close to the body throughout the drill. Instructors allow the next player in line to begin the drill as soon as the player ahead has moved out of range.

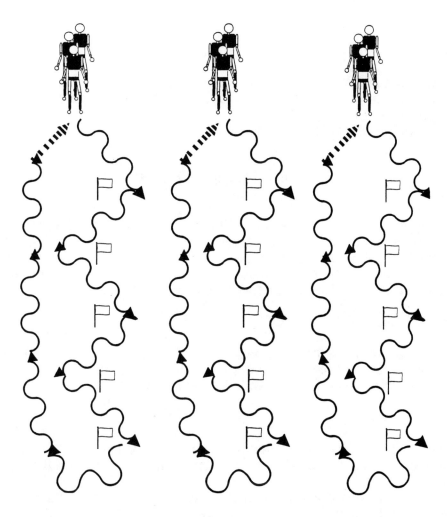

Fig. 6.2

Role of Player

1. Move through the obstacles as quickly as possible while maintaining control.
2. Use the inside and outside of both feet.
3. Accelerate throughout the activity.

Role of Instructor

1. Encourage quick movements while maintaining control, which is paramount in this exercise.
2. Ensure a limited waiting time for players.
3. Don't include 10 or more cones or flags in the drill. The repetition comes from practicing the drill several times.
4. Increase or decrease the distance between markers depending on the success of the player.

Performance Benefits of Dribbling Through Markers

1. Forces a player to alter the directions while using both feet.
2. Provides opportunities for the player to use the outside and inside portions of the foot.
3. Allows the player to move at his/her own pace.

Drill Number Three

Dribbling with Defensive Pressure: The structure of this drill is the same as drill number one, but 3 or 4 defensive players are added to the grid area. As dribbling players move about the grid, the defensive players are attempting to steal the ball. If a player loses possession, he/she become a defensive player and the defensive player becomes an attacker.

Role of Player

1. Move around the grid with head up and eyes on defensive players.
2. Maintain control of the ball keeping it close to the feet.
3. Use both feet and feinting skills to maintain possession.

Role of Instructor

1. Encourage continual movement from each player.
2. Switch defensive players who remain in that role for more than one minute.
3. Increase or decrease the size of the grid depending on the success or failure of the players.

Performance Benefits of Dribbling with Defensive Pressure

1. Forces the dribbling player to react under defensive pressure.
2. Encourages a player to keep his/her head up and view the surroundings.
3. Creates a pressure situation that encourages the player to continue moving around the grid, using both feet, and implementing various inventive movement patterns.

Specific Dribbling Techniques

Specific techniques are associated with the skill of dribbling. This section will introduce four specific dribbling techniques created by Van Balkom (1986). Each dribble technique is helpful for a player to build a foundation essential for success on the field. The methods are: (1) The Foundation, (2) The V Move, (3) The Single Scissors, and (4) The Twist.

Teaching Points for The Foundation

1. Move with the ball in the direction of the opponent.
2. Pass the ball with the outside of the foot behind the opponent.
3. Push with the passing foot and move around the opponent.
4. Collect and control the ball on the other side.

Photos 6.3 - 6.5

Teaching Points for The V Move

1. Move the ball in the direction of the opponent.
2. When approximately 2 to 3 feet away, step on the ball with the sole of the foot.
3. Draw it back toward the body.
4. Pivot off the balance or standing leg.
5. With inside of the foot push it past the opponent.

Photos 6.6 - 6.8

Teaching Points for The Single Scissors

1. Move the ball in the direction of the opponent.
2. When one is about one or two yards away (depending on the speed),
3. take a large step and circle your foot around the ball.
4. Transfer the weight onto the foot that has moved around the ball.
5. Push the ball past opponent with the outside of the opposite foot.

Photos 6.9 - 6.10

Teaching Points for the The Twist

1. As one approaches the opponent, change the dribbling angle to one side, forcing the defender to intercept the run.
2. As the defender moves into position,
3. simultaneously pivot off the balance leg and drag the ball across the body with the opposite leg in the opposite direction.
4. Push off that leg then tap the ball with the inside of the opposite foot into open space.

Photos 6.12 - 6.14

The skill of dribbling is an art. Players can develop and apply their own individuality and charisma to every dribbling technique. These four dribbling methods can be used as a springboard to develop others. Players should not try to practice too many techniques, but limit their concentration to two or three. Once they have mastered these methods, combined with their own creativity and imagination on the ball, a player will find himself/herself beating opponents and generating space or scoring opportunities.

Chapter Seven

Principles of Individual, Group, and Team Attacking Tactics

Players who apply the appropriate attacking techniques of passing, trapping, and shooting, will not be as successful in game situations unless they understand and execute proper attacking tactics. Assessment and comprehension of the actions and movements of players surrounding the ball during team possession is paramount to goal scoring. Accurate decision making will dictate either shot on goal or loss of possession. When a player achieves ball possession, multiple decisions are available. Should a player with the ball pass, shoot, or dribble? Should teammates move forward or back in supporting roles? Should a player move away from the ball, opening up space for the ball carrier, or close in to provide an optional passing opportunity? Appropriate and suitable decisions pertaining to the options listed above are just as important as the proper and consistent execution of individual techniques. Understanding and applying the appropriate individual, group, and team tactics in attack are foundationally important for each player.

Individual Tactics in Attack

Initiation of movement by attacking players stem from one specific area, the location of the teammate with the ball. All movements, forward in advance or backward in support, are based from the position of the ball handler. Individual tactics originate and manifest from here. They are divided into three distinct groups: first attacker, second attacker, and third attacker.

The first attacker is the most dangerous person on the field. He/she is the player with the ball. This player initiates movement, makes decisions, and applies the proper attacking method as dictated by the defense he/she is encountering.

Skills of the First Attacker

The player who knows when and how to apply the appropriate attacking techniques are considered to have skill. The skills of the first attacker include the following:

1. **Controlling:** (a) knowing how to gain possession, (b) positioning himself/herself to intercept a pass or steal the ball from an opposing player, (c) which trapping (stopping the ball with either the foot, chest, or part of the leg) technique should be applied, and (d) anticipating what to do with the ball during possession.

2. **Passing**: Imparting the appropriate pass as dictated by the situation on the field and the movements of teammates.

3. **Shooting**: Viewing the options and determining the type, angle, and location of the shot.

4. **Dribbling**: The final choice for any attacker should be dribbling the ball. Again, the field location where possession has been won will dictate the dribbling options (if a player elects to dribble).

5. **Heading**: Heading is another option a player can use as the first attacker. Implementing the appropriate technique with accuracy will make this an effective option depending on the situation created.

Skills of the Second Attacker

The second attacker, the player positioned nearest the first attacker, is considered the supporting player. This player is vital to the success of a team. He/she creates multiple attacking options for the first attacker. The responsibilities of the second attacker include:

1. **Attacking support**: (a) providing the first attacker with the option to move the ball forward with a pass or dribble, or (b) pass the ball back depending on the position and configuration of the opposing players. The second attacker helps to ensure team possession.

2. **Defensive support**: If the first attacker loses control of the ball, the second attacker can move in and become the primary defender.

3. **Direction**: The second attacker is responsible for providing direction for the first attacker. The position of the second attacker allows greater field vision. The attacker has the opportunity to observe the movements of teammates and opposing players. Verbal reinforcement will help the first attacker make decisions on passing, dribbling, or shooting.

4. **Proper Positioning**: The position of the second attacker is critical for a successful outcome. Depending on the location of the first attacker, the second attacker should place himself/herself at a right angle (45 degrees is most desired) or directly behind first attacker. Discovering the correct distance away from the first defender is also critical. In the attacking third of the field (where risks should be taken) the player should be positioned between 5 and 10 yards away. In the middle third where few risks should be taken, approximately 10 to 15 yards away is sufficient. Finally, in the defensive third, where no risks should be taken, a distance of 15 to 30 yards is recommended.

Skills of the Third Attacker

The skills of the third attacker are essential for developing and creating space for the first attacker. A player who is the third attacker is the one who imparts the creative and unpredictable movements of a team. By disguising the intentions and forcing defensive players to open up gaps, goal scoring opportunities will develop. The skills of the third attacker should include the following:

1. **Overlapping Runs**: A Run made from behind the first attacker

2. **Diagonal Penetrating Run**: Movements into the middle of the field and toward the goal.

3. **Blind Side Runs**: A run made behind the defender.

4. **Dummy Runs**: A run that is made to pull the defender away from a marked teammate (someone who is covered by an opposing player) or area of the field.

A player who consistently executes all the skills involved in individual attacking tactics will maintain ball possession while developing scoring opportunities for teammates. Knowing when and how to initiate the specific movements or impart the proper technique leads teams to goal scoring chances.

Group Tactics

During a game situation it will become obvious to the spectator that successful soccer players effectively utilize the group situations that occur around the ball. If possession is won in the attacking third of the field, two midfielders and a forward may come in close contact with each other. The concluding result of what happens with the ball, whether it's shot on goal or lost to the opposing team, will depend on how the players react and how successful they are in their attempts.

Players who disguise their intentions create scoring opportunities. When possession has been won the entire team is on the attack. The movements of players near and away from the ball will dictate if a scoring opportunity will manifest. Movements by players around the ball will direct the actions of the player with the ball. The ball carrier needs to be aware of his/her surroundings. The purpose of movement is to generate open space. This is the space that is not occupied by another player or opponent. If an attacker moves into a space ahead of the player with the ball, and a defender follows, the space the player has left has just become open. This is space other attacking players can utilize. If an attacking player moves into open space and no defender follows, the player with the ball can utilize the space by passing to the open player. The movements of the open players around the ball should be unpredictable and creative. There is no standard prescription to follow. A run without the ball should be clever and deceptive, and a ball handler needs to adapt to the situations created by teammates.

The Overlapping Run

When a player moves forward from a position behind a ball handler, ahead into the open space in front, he/she has performed the overlapping run (See Figure 7.1).

Fig. 7.1

A player making this type of run must consider the following:

1. Does the space he/she left place the team in any danger, especially if possession is immediately lost?
2. At what time will making the run be most effective? This will be determined by the opponents movements.
3. Communicate to the player with the ball when to either hold or make a pass.

Once the decision has been made to pass the ball to the overlapping player, the player who made the pass must quickly decide either to support the overlapping player (becoming the second attacker), or move across field. This move might deceive a defensive player, creating open space for other teammates. A player passing the ball during this situation should consider the following:

1. **Accuracy of the pass**: It is critical for a player to pass the ball accurately. Assess where the overlapping player will be, then passing to that spot. Instructors are to observe inexperienced players. Often, they will make passes where a player was, not where they will be.

2. **The timing of the pass**: Sometimes a player will hesitate to make a pass. This allows opponents time to cover or close down the attacking player moving into open space. Other times a player will pass too soon, thereby disallowing the run to develop.

3. **The speed or pace of the pass**: A passing player needs to consider how much power should be imparted on the ball. Sometimes a player puts too much speed on the ball which makes it difficult to control. Other times passers strike the ball too softly. This action permits a defensive player to intercept the pass, or force the receiving player to slow his/her run and come back to the ball.

Diagonal Penetrating Run

Another type of run, the diagonal run (Figure 7.2), is initiated by a player who runs diagonally toward the center of the field. These runs are most dangerous when made from the middle or attacking thirds of the field. Running into open space toward the middle of the field will cause great alarm for opponents. The intent is to have a player quickly move into the middle toward the goal. He/she then receives a pass from a teammate, which opens up a scoring opportunity. This will depend on the location and defensive arrangement at the time of ball reception.

Fig. 7.2

Blind Side Run

During game situations space is often found behind the defending player. This space between the defender and the goal is an area in which a player should take advantage. When offensive players move into the open space behind a defender, it is considered a blindside run or backdoor run (Figure 7.3). The defender cannot see the movement. Thus its name, the blind side run.

When players make the blind side run, the attacking player with the ball will be able to see the movement of his/her teammate and make the decision whether to pass or not to that player. A player making the blindside run should consider the following:

1. The position of the attacking players.
2. The opponents position.
3. The area of the field where the ball is located.
4. What advantage is it for the team to move into that area.

Fig. 7.3

Disguise "Dummy" Run

Another method for creating space is the disguise or dummy run (Figure 7.4). This occurs when one player runs into a specific area to draw defenders away from the ball or sections of the field. This can open up space for another teammate, or the ball carrier. A player making this type of run disguises intentions, draws defenders in his/her direction, and provides teammates with multiple options. This strategy is very effective in all thirds of the field, but extremely dangerous for opposing players when successfully performed in the attacking third. Players performing this run should consider the following:

1. The timing of the run.
2. The position of the defenders and teammate with the ball.
3. The direction of the run, ensuring you don't draw multiple defenders toward the ball carrier.
4. The pace of the run, disguising intentions.

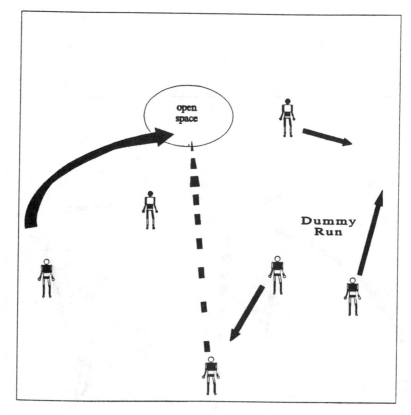

Fig. 7.4

Five Attacking Principles in Team Tactics

When possession is achieved, the first essential action of each player is to space himself/herself out. A team that is on attack must move players into positions on the field that give them enough space to work the ball. The more space a player has from the opponents, the more time he/she will have to control, pass, dribble, or shoot the ball. A major premise in team tactics rests on the concept of space and time. Each one of the five principles of team tactics is intended to create areas where players will have space and time to work the ball. Space refers to the amount of area a player will have away from opposing players. Time is a result of space control. If space is available, he/she will have time with the ball. The five principles in attacking tactics include: Width, Depth, Mobility, Improvision, and Penetration.

Width

Width is a principle that encourages the defense to separate and spread out (Figure 7.5). When possession is achieved, attacking players should disconnect and move into open spaces. This will provide passing opportunities for the teammate with the ball. If a fullback wins the ball,

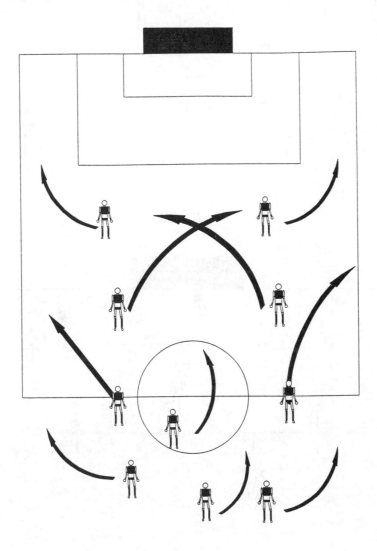

others should move into support and attacking positions behind, to the side, and in front of the ball carrier. If a pass cannot be made forward, play the ball back to a supporting player. Offering several passing opportunities for the player with the ball should be the focal point for the team. As attacking players move apart from each other, opposing players often follow, thereby creating gaps and open spaces (Figure 7.6). This diagram demonstrates when players are spread out across the field. This is **Width**. In contrast, if players move in toward each other (Figure 7.7), space is limited. A successful pass will be difficult in this situation. In figure 7.6, players are spread out, forcing the defensive players to pull out, away from their goal. This opens up a greater number of passing and scoring opportunities.

Fig 7.5

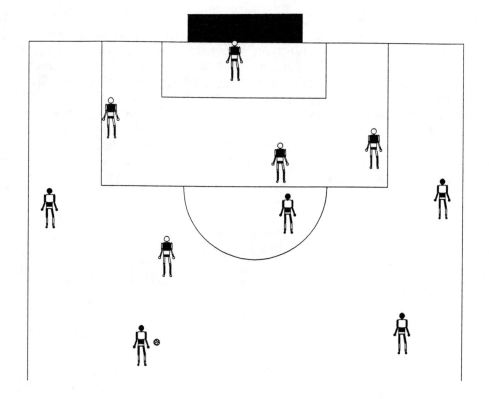

Fig. 7.6

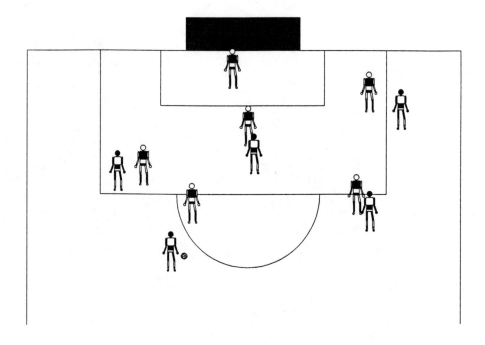

Fig. 7.7

Depth

The second principle in attack is **depth**. Depth reflects the level of support given to a player with the ball. When successfully performed this concept will increase the number of passing angles, options, and help in maintaining possession. Frequently, a ball is won near opposing players. Once the ball is controlled, players must move into support positions and become second and third attackers. A supporting player must position himself/herself about 10 to 15 yards away. This depends on the area where the ball is located.

Often a player will move too close to his/her teammates. When the ball is passed, the opposing player marking the ball carrier will have an easier time to close down the space between the player with the ball. The ground will also dictate the distance of the support. If the ground is bumpy or fast, the supporting player may want to give himself/herself more time and space to control the ball.

The angle or location of the supporting player is also important. Supporting players must be positioned where a teammate can pass the ball without being intercepted. The more "square" (parallel) he/she is with teammate (Figure 7.8), the more one has limited the passing angle. Notice how the players are caught square with the ball carrier in figure 7.8. The player with the ball has limited passing opportunities. Yet, in figure 7.9, player (a) has moved back in a supporting role, while player (b) has moved forward. The ball carrier now has two passing opportunities.

Fig. 7.8

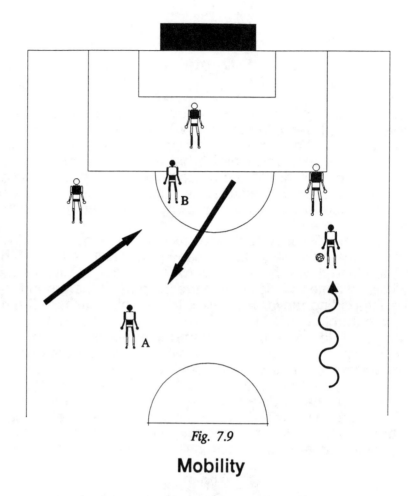

Fig. 7.9

Mobility

Mobility, the third principle during attack, refers to the interplay of roles and responsibilities. Players move into situations that require other players to leave their responsibilities and help each other. All players, whether in attack or defense, must be willing to take on the responsibilities of his/her teammates. If an outside fullback moves forward on a run down the flank, an outside midfielder may need to drop back to cover for the overlapping fullback. As with the diagram below (Figure 7.10), player (a) moves forward in an overlapping run. This move encourages player (b) to cover.

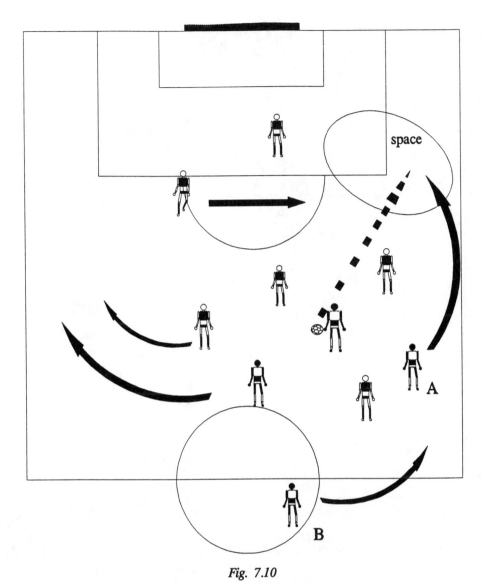

Fig. 7.10

Improvision

   The fourth principle in attack is **improvision**. This occurs when a player interjects creativity and ingenuity on the field. The movements of a player near and away from other teammates will help create passing and scoring opportunities. A player who makes "disguise" runs (drawing defenders away from a situation), or overlapping runs. With the example below (Figure 7.11), two players are attempting to move defensive players away form the middle of the field. This move creates a one on one situation with the ball carrier. If the defender is beaten, a great scoring opportunity will exist.

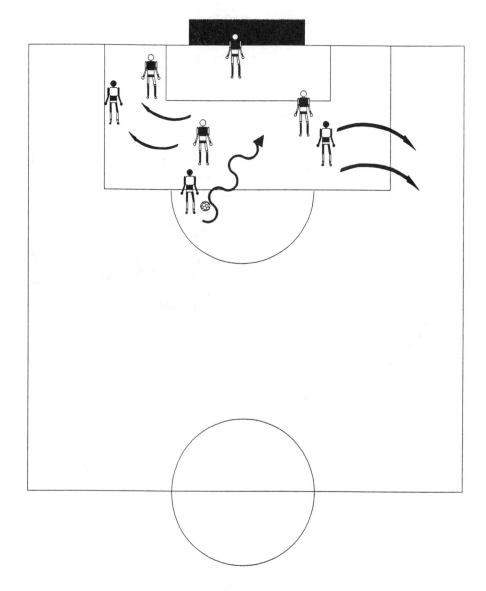

Fig. 7.11

Penetration

The final principle for team attacking tactics is **penetration**. When two or more passing opportunities exist, the player with the ball should choose the one that will result in the most penetration into the defense (Figure 7.12). Passing the ball into the center of the defense will generate fear and concern for defenders. Players making penetrating runs should position themselves close to the goal. In the figure below, the ball carrier has several passing opportunities. The one that would create the most penetration and concern is number two. A pass to that teammate places an attacker with a ball very close to the goal.

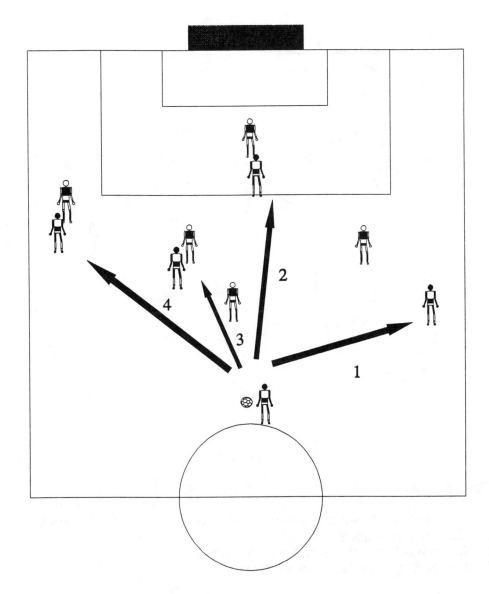

Fig. 7.12

Drills to Develop Attacking Tactics

Drill Number One

Build to End-line: This drill is played on half a soccer field. Seven attackers are paired against four field defenders and two positioned on the end-line. The attackers are attempting to build an attack and move the ball down the field. The object is to place the ball on the end-line by beating all field and end-line defenders. The drill starts with one attacker passing the ball into the field of play. Instructors are to encourage players to perform various tactical runs while reinforcing the concepts of width and support.

130

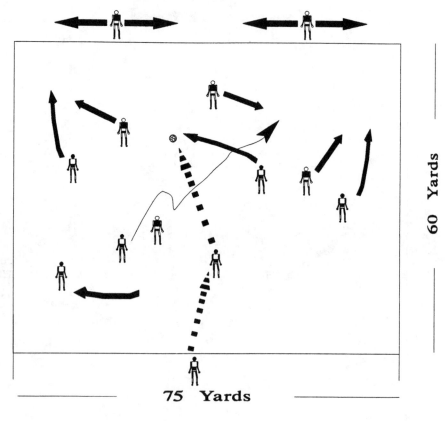

Fig. 7.13

Role of Player

1. Implement movement patterns that open up space for teammates.
2. Disguise intentions.
3. Move the ball with short controlled passes.
4. Support teammates after each pass.

Role of Instructor

1. Verbalize the need for width, penetration, improvision, support, and depth.
2. Encourage continuous movement and mobility.
3. Maintain an abundant supply of balls to keep the drill going.
4. Modify by removing the end-line defenders with two small goals.

Performance Benefits of Build to End-line

1. Teaches many of the tactical aspects of attack.
2. Moves players forward toward an established objective.
3. Creates a game related situation that can be quickly stopped if instruction is required.

Drill Number Two

Four Goal Soccer: This drill is played on a field 75 yards wide and 75 yards long. Four goals are placed on each end-line and side-line. Two teams of 8 or 12 are positioned on the field. Each team will shoot on two goals. One on the end-line and one on the side-line. Play begins when the instructor kicks a ball into play.

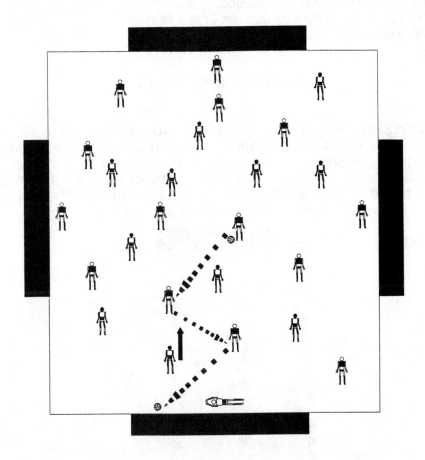

Fig. 7.14

Role of Player

1. Utilize the entire field to maintain possession and create a scoring opportunity.
2. Quickly move to open space and disguise intentions.
3. Focus on one and two-touch passing.
4. Search and pass to the open player in goal scoring range.
5. Shoot quickly, don't hesitate when given the opportunity.

Role of Instructor

1. Encourage the player to generate open spaces for teammates.
2. Emphasize quick decisive passes that place players in scoring situations.
3. Reinforce all tactical concepts of attack.
4. Maintain an abundant supply of balls close by.

Performance Benefits of Four Goal Soccer

1. Teaches various attacking tactics.
2. Encourages the player to use the entire field.
3. Develops a balanced field of play.

Drill Number Three

Man Marking Drill: Players are divided into two groups of 10 to 12. Play is conducted on a regulation size soccer field. The object is to score goals. The design of the drill is to teach man-on-man marking. Every player is instructed to locate and mark one man for the entire drill. If someone is forced to tackle or mark another player, the team who lost the ball gains a free kick. Focus on a buildup from one end to the other.

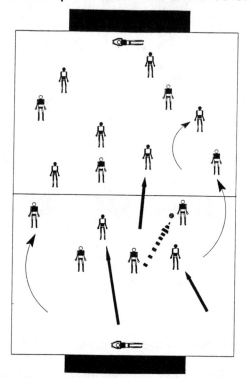

Fig. 7.15

Role of Player

1. Maintain a tight marking position.
2. Only pull away from opponent as a last resort.
3. Once possession is gained, quickly move into a counter attack.
4. Apply individual and group tactical moves to break from opposition.

Role of Instructor

1. Enforce the rule of marking only one player.
2. Encourage a quick transition for attack to defense.
3. Reinforce control and restraint to allow sufficient time to reposition.

Performance Benefits of Man Marking Drill

1. Prepares players for marking situations.
2. Teaches group and team tactics in both attack and defense.
3. Provides a realistic picture of a game situation.

Chapter Eight

Defensive Skills and Techniques

Introduction

Each soccer player should develop sound defensive skills and techniques no matter where he/she is positioned on the field during the start of the game. In chapter three we learned that when a team gains possession of a ball each player on that side is on attack. Likewise, when a team loses possession, each player on that side is on defense. Often times instructors mistakenly call fullbacks or back players defenders, in reality, every one is a defender and everyone is an attacker, it depends on who has possession of the ball.

Successful defensive play requires the application of physical and mental capabilities. Physical skills include proper tackling, positioning, supporting, tracking, and movement. Mental skills involve attributes of patience, concentration, and discipline. Instructors working with soccer players should focus training sessions that improve both physical and mental skills.

In this section, specific skills of body stance, positioning, and tackling are discussed and accompanied with drills patterned to nurture the development of each physical and mental defensive techniques.

Individual Defensive Skills and Techniques

Defensive Stance

The appropriate physical stance a player assumes is critical when confronting an opposing player with the ball. When a player finds himself/herself on defense and marking a ball carrier, he/she must be able to react to the quick moves and feints of the opposing player.

The defensive stance is designed to help a player quickly react to the movements of the opposition (See Photo 8.1). The proper method involves four parts: (1) feet shoulders width apart with one foot placed slightly in front of the other, (2) weight of the body supported by the balls of the feet, (3) knees bent, and (4) head down with eyes on the ball.

Correct positioning of the defensive player can dictate the movement of the ball carrier. When a defensive player is confronting the opponent in possession of the ball, the player must remember 7 significant components:

1. try not to let the opposing player turn the ball towards your goal,
2. quickly close down the space between yourself and the attacker,
3. don't position too close or too far away from the opposing player,
4. stay goal side (position yourself between the goal and the ball),
5. be patient,
6. use fainting skills in an effort to get the attacker to commit, and
7. attempt to make the tackle when the attacking player attempts to turn and face the goal you are defending.

Photo 8.1

The first priority of the defensive player is to not allow the attacking player to turn and face the goal. This requires the defensive player to be positioned close enough to provide appropriate pressure but not too far to where the opposing player can turn with the ball and face the goal. Generally this position is about 3 to 4 feet.

As the defender moves toward the correct distance he/she should assume the proper defensive stance previously mentioned. Once this position is established, the defender should initiate feints that encourage the attacker to commit. Being patient and concentrating on the ball are critical for success of the defender. Once a defender has over committed or moved in too quickly, they are usually beaten.

When the ball carrier has committed to a specific direction or he/she have lost touch with the ball, the defender can move in with a tackle. According to Wade (1981), an effective tackler possesses four specific attributes that lead defensive players to consistent and successful outcomes in tackling attempts.

Attribute Number One: The first is to focus on the ball and refuse to be tempted into making a move or commitment because of the attacker's deception and trickery. You need to be convinced the ball can be won or knocked away.

Attribute Number Two: The second involves not over committing to the ball (diving in with full force and weight) which puts a player off balance and in a situation where he/she can't recover swift enough to defend. Be quick in and out of the tackle, maintaining bodily control and balance by stabilizing on the balls of the feet.

Attribute Number Three: The third includes determination and never giving up. If you are consistently fooled and deceived, adjust ones approach and try something different. If you are beaten down the flank (sides of the field), channel the ball carrier to the middle.

Attribute Number Four: The fourth and final trait is to defend with courage. Never give an opponent a free and unchallenged chance to play the ball whether it is on the ground or in the air. "Above all, never, never give in" (Wade, 1981).

Three types of tackles are used when players move in and make attempts on the ball. The front block tackle, side block tackle, or the sliding tackle. Depending on the situation or ball location on the field, a player will apply one of the three methods listed above.

Front Block Tackle

The front block tackle is a tackling method used when confronting an opponent head on. When a player initiates this type of tackle, commitment to the tackle should occur when he/she is confident the ball can be won.

Teaching Points for the Front Block Tackle

1. Keep eyes on the ball.
2. Maintain correct defensive stance, knees bent, one foot in front of the other about shoulders width apart, weight on the balls of the feet.
3. Lean slightly forward.
4. Maintain a low center of gravity.
5. Ankle of the tackling foot is rigid.
6. Drive the tackling foot into the ball.
7. Contact the center portion of the ball.
8. Drive the ball through and past the opponent.
9. Collect the ball.

Photo 8.2 - 8.3

Common Faults and Corrections

Fault

Your tackle lacks power and firmness, and the ball is not won.

Correction

1. Tackle the ball with courage, driving foot into the center portion of ball.
2. Keep the ankle rigid and stiff.
3. Drive your foot into the ball and past the foot of your opponent.

Fault

Defender makes contact with the ball but fails to push away from the attacker.

Correction

1. Aggressively make forceful contact with the center portion of the ball.
2. Maintain a rigid and stiff ankle throughout the tackle.
3. Don't hesitate, move in quickly while maintaining eye contact with the ball.

Drills to Develop the Front Block Tackle

These two drills are designed to introduce players to the front block tackle. Appropriate teaching progressions are important when instructors are teaching players, especially young players, in tackling techniques; techniques that can be dangerous and cause injury. Players are encouraged to start slow and then progress with increased force and determination during the tackling drills, but safety should always come first.

Drill Number One

Partner Support Tackle: A stationary ball is placed between two partners who have put their hands on each others shoulders while keeping their arms straight. Both players are asked to simultaneously tackle the stationary ball with the front block tackle in a slow and gentle fashion.

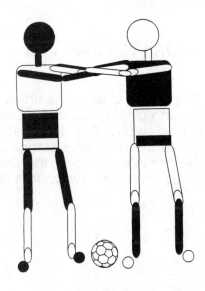

Fig. 8.1

After players have begun to understand the correct technique, the instructor can modify the situation by having players drop their hands and lower their shoulders. The situation is the same, two players between a stationary ball, but the players are now encouraged to generate a low center of gravity by bending their knees and power into the tackle. Lowering one's body will help a player maintain balance and keep control of his/her own body during contact.

Role of Tackler

1. Move through the action slowly.
2. Work with a partner, not against him/her.
3. As you become proficient and confident, increase the power and determination in each tackle while maintaining safe environment.

Role of Instructor

1. Encourage the player to experiment.
2. Pair up players of equal size, weight, and experience.
3. Ensure the player is progressively increasing the power and force after he/she has consistently demonstrated the appropriate technique.

Performance Benefits of Partner Support Tackle

1. Introduces the technique in a safe environment.
2. Allows the player to self discover the technique.
3. Allows a player to advance at his/her own pace while increasing the force and power of the tackle.

Drill Number Two

Block Tackle a Moving Opponent: During this drill a ball carrier is placed 5 to 10 yards from the defending player. Upon a signal, the attacker dribbles at a slow pace toward the defender. The defender moves in the direction of the attacker and assumes the defensive stance when he/she is 3 to 4 feet away. As the attacker makes a move, the defender is to attempt a block tackle and win the ball. Roles are switched after each attempt.

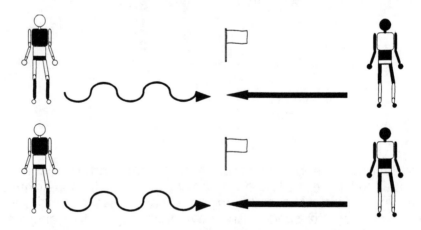

Fig. 8.2

Role of Tackler

1. Close down the distance between player and attacker, initiate the tackle at the appropriate time.
2. Keep eyes on the ball, utilize the appropriate technique.

Role of Instructor

1. Ensure the attacker moves at a slow pace.
2. Increase or decrease the distance and speed of the attack depending on the success of the player.
3. Ensure safety by allowing a player to progress at a slow pace.
4. Pair partners up appropriately.

Performance Benefits of Block Tackle a Moving Opponent

1. To increase the challenge in tackling.
2. Provides a player an opportunity to perfect the block tackle while participating in moving situation.

The Side Block Tackle

In game situations defending players may approach a ball carrier from the side. When this occurs the defending player can initiate the side block tackle to steal or knock the ball away. This technique is an effective tackling move that all players on the field should master.

Teaching Points to the Side Block Tackle

1. Approach the attacker from the side.
2. Keep a low center of gravity to maintain bodily control and balance.
3. Keep eyes focused on the ball.
4. Plant balanced leg (non tackling leg) next to the leg of the dribbler.
5. Lower center of gravity by bending the knee of the non-tackling leg, and swing the tackling leg around and into the ball.
6. Use the instep of the tackling leg to make contact with the ball.
7. Drive the instep into and though the center of the ball.
8. Maintain balance and keep on feet.

Photo 8.4 - 8.5

Common Faults and Corrections

Fault

Attacker maintains possession of the ball.

Correction

1. When driving the instep into and though the mid-line of the ball don't pull back or hesitate.
2. Firmly plant the balance or non-tackling leg near the leg of the attacker.
3. Maintain balance and stay on feet.

Fault

He/she fouled the player with the ball.

Correction

1. Keep eyes on the ball and make powerful contact on the middle portion of the ball.
2. Hold arms out for balance, don't place hands on the opponent or fall into him/her during the tackle.

A Drill to Develop The Side Block Tackle

Side Block Tackle with Partner: During this drill, players are positioned 5 yards apart with one partner having a soccer ball. On the signal, the attacking player with the ball is asked to dribble forward at half speed while the tackling player parallel from the attacker moves across diagonally and attempts the side block tackle. After each attempt the partners rotate.

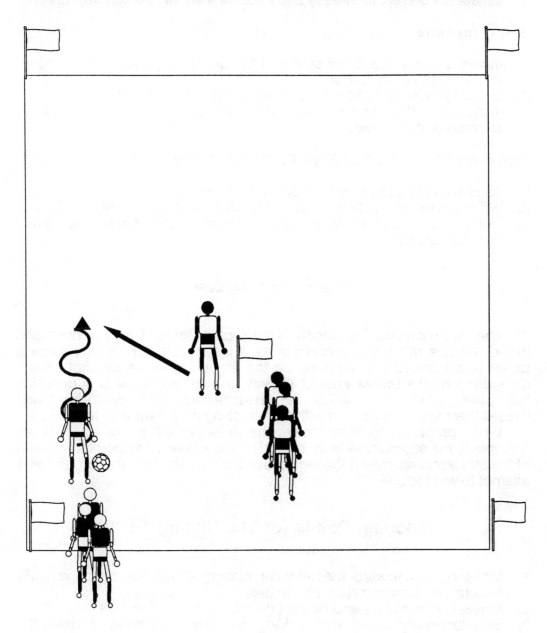

Fig. 8.3

Role of Player

1. The player with the ball is to move at a slow pace, allowing the tackling partner the opportunity to practice the side block tackle with limited challenge from the attacker.
2. The tackling partner is to close down the distance between the dribble and himself/herself as quickly as possible.
3. Initiate the correct technique and make adjustments when appropriate.

Role of Instructor

1. Increase or decrease the speed of the attacking player depending on the success of the tackler.
2. Ensure proper classification or pairing of partners for safety.
3. Increase or decrease the distance of the partners depending of the success of the tackler.

Performance Benefits of Side Block Tackle with Partner

1. To allow a player to progress at him/her own pace.
2. Will help ensure safety while learning the correct technique.
3. Creates a situation where the instructor can furnish feedback instantaneously.

The Sliding Tackle

The third tackle used in soccer is the sliding tackle. It is recommended that defenders utilize this technique as a last resort during play since a player is committed and ends up on the ground after the attempt. If the defender wins the ball or knocks it away, the sliding tackle is successful, but often when the tackle is unsuccessful, the defender finds himself/herself on the ground with the attacking player moving forward.

When preparing to slide tackle, the defender will move as close as possible to the attacker, slide in, extending the whole body across the path of the attacker, and sweep the leg across and into the ball, making the final attempt to win the ball.

Teaching Points for The Sliding Tackle

1. Move quickly toward the attacker closing down the distance while maintaining concentration on the ball.
2. Maintain composure and bodily control.
3. Simultaneously bend non-tackling leg while lowering it onto the ground, using it as a pad to slide on.
4. Swing the tackling leg (top leg) into the path of the attacker.

5. Ankle of the tackling leg should be slightly dorsi flexed (toe pointing up in a cup shaped fashion)
6. The instep of the foot should drive into the mid-line portion of the ball.
7. Trap or knock the ball away for the opponent.
8. Return to feet.

Photos 8.6 - 8.8

Common Faults and Corrections

Fault

Contact is made on the attacker, not the ball.

Correction

1. Concentrate and focus eyes on the ball throughout the entire technique.
2. Maintain proper distance from the ball carrier.

Fault

Contact is made on the ball, but the attacker has maintained possession.

Correction

1. Swing the tackling leg into the ball with force and power.
2. Move in with determination and perseverance, don't hold back.
3. Make a solid connection with foot onto the mid-line portion of the ball.
4. Maintain a dorsi flexed (cupped position) on the ankle of the tackling leg.

Fault

The opponent with the ball is fouled.

Correction

1. Don't make contact from behind, but slide ahead of the attacker and swing leg around in front of him/her. Make contact with ball first.
2. Attempt to avoid any contact with the attacker.

The sliding tackle is a fun and exciting tackling method to execute, but can be hazardous for the attacker and defender. When practicing the sliding tackle instructors should place players on a section of the field that is soft with high grass. This will help maintain safety while maximizing the sliding potential. Hard and dry surfaces may lead to injuries, especially when introducing the sliding tackle to players who have never been properly instructed in the technique.

Drills and Activities to Develop Each Tackling Techniques

After each player has learned the basic concepts of each tackling technique, instructors are encouraged to create situations that allow the player to practice each method in a game related situations.

Drills should be designed to challenge the player while allowing multiple opportunities or repetitions for practice. Instructors are encouraged to place their instructional focus on the cue, the specific component desired to be learned, which in this case a specified tackling technique.

Drill Number One

Dribble to the End-line: During this drill two players with one ball are positioned in a grid area 10x20. The object is for one partner to dribble the ball to the opposite end-line while the opposing partner is attempting to steal the ball or knock it out of bounds. After each exchange, the partners switch roles. Three points are awarded for the player who beats the defender and dribbles, under control, to the opposing end-line. One point is awarded for each time the defender knocks the ball out of bounds or steals the ball. Instructors are encouraged to ask the defending player to position himself/herself in the middle of the grid area before approaching the player with the ball. Once the player with the ball moves forward, the defending player can make a move.

Fig. 8.4

Role of Defending Player

1. Close down the distance between the defender and the ball carrier as quickly as possible.
2. Maintain composure, keep balance, and be patient.

Role of Instructor

1. Pair players on size, weight, ability, and experience to help maintain a safe environment.
2. Provide proper supervision and make appropriate adjustments when tackling techniques are improperly executed.

Performance Benefits of Dribbling to the end-line

1. Potential to utilizes all tackling techniques during a modified game situation.
2. To allows multiple tackling opportunities for leading players to mastery in each tackling technique.
3. To provide a competitive situation that encourages a player to work hard while practicing each tackling technique.

Drill Number Two

Steal the Ball: This drill includes three players. Two players with a ball are positioned inside a 10x10 yard grid while a third player is stationed outside the grid. Upon a signal, the two players inside the grid are playing keep away, one attempting to steal the ball while the other strives to maintain possession. The player positioned outside the grid is a counter. When a player has lost possession for 15 seconds or the ball is kicked or knocked outside the grid, the players change roles. The outside player switches with the defender after a minute of play. Points can be awarded to players who maintain possession for over 15 seconds.

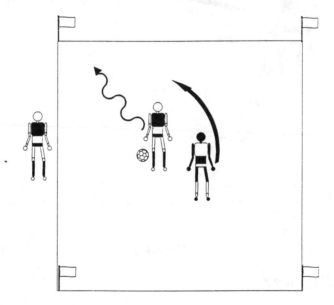

Fig. 8.5

Role of Defender

1. Utilize various tackling techniques to win the ball.
2. Be patient, don't overcommit.
3. Strive to stay on feet.

Role of Instructor

1. Pair participants based on size, weight, and experience.
2. Provide proper supervision, maintain a safe environment.

Performance Benefits of Steal the Ball

1. To provide multiple opportunities to practice the various tackling techniques.
2. To create a competitive but fun environment.
3. To allow a player to work and learn at his/her own pace if appropriately paired.

Drill Number Three

Cat and Mouse: This drill involves 12 players, 8 attackers each with a soccer ball, and 4 defenders. The object during the drill is for the defenders to tackle and steal a ball away from one of the attackers while each ball carrier is moving and dribbling around a 30 x 30 grid area. Once a defender steals a ball from one of the attackers they switch roles, the attacker becomes the defender and the defender becomes the attacker.

Fig. 8.6

Role of Defender

1. Locate an attacker and pursue that player.
2. Execute the appropriate tackling technique as dictated by the situation.
3. Once a player steals a ball, he/she should accelerate into open space, keeping head up, viewing his/her surroundings, and maintaining control and possession of the ball.

Role of Instructor

1. Encourage the defenders to pursue with determination and tackle with confidence.
2. Reinforce the proper tackling techniques.
3. Switch a defender if a player has not won a ball after one minute.

Performance Benefits of Cat and Mouse

1. Requires defenders to pursue, close down, and tackle a moving player.
2. To encourage consistent challenges and concentration.
3. To increase fitness levels while improving tackling skills.

Drill Number Four

Support and Cover: This drill is played with four players in a 10x10 yards grid. Two defenders are facing two attackers. The object is to develop skills of support and cover. As the two attackers pass the ball between themselves, the defenders switch roles of first and second defender. The first defender is marking the ball carrier, while the second defender covers. This continues for three or four passes. When the whistle is blown, the defenders attempt to stop the attackers from scoring on goal.

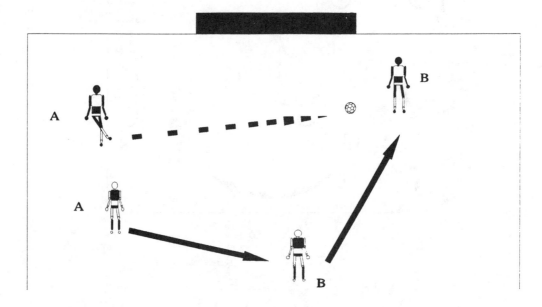

Role of Defender

1. Quickly move into a covering position and maintain defensive stance.
2. Body position is critical.
3. Check angle and distance when supporting first defender.
4. At whistle, first defender should patiently wait for the tackling opportunity.
5. Second defender, be ready to move in when needed.

Role of Instructor

1. Verbalize the quick role change between the two defenders.
2. Check positioning; make changes when needed.
3. Maintain the focus of support and cover after whistle is blown.

Performance Benefits of Support and Cover

1. Reinforces all tackling skills while introducing group defensive tactics.
2. Teaches the roles of first and second defender.
3. Places players in a competitive situation while developing basic defensive skills.

Principles of Individual and Team Defensive Tactics

Introduction

In Chapter Eight we learned that when a team loses possession of the ball each player is automatically on defense. The players field position is irrelevant. Each player is responsible for defending the goal. Reactions toward the responsibility change from offense to defense must be immediate. Individual defenders should attempt to make the play of ball handlers predictable. Forcing them into certain areas of the field and away from your goal.

This chapter is divided into two distinct sections. The first section lists the individual tactics of the first and second defender. The second section discusses the five defensive tactics used in regaining possession.

Individual Tactics in Defense

The First Defender

The first defender is the player closest to the ball handler. This defensive player has one major objective, Take the ball from the opposition. This requires an aggressive, skillful, and determined individual.

Skills of the First Defender

Each player during the game will become the first defender at some point. This requires each player to understand and learn the appropriate strategies and responsibilities of the first defender. Applying these concepts will help ensure a safe and successful defense of his/her goal. The six defensive skills of the first defender include the following:

1. Close down the space between defender and the attacker.
2. Keep the attacker from turning toward the goal.
3. Pressure the attacker with the ball.
4. Make the movements and play of the attacker predictable.
5. Keep goal side of the attacker.
6. Tackle or intercept the ball.

Applying the Six Skills of the First Defender

The first skill, "closing down the space between the first defender and attacker with the ball," refers to shortening the space created between the two opposing players. The first defender should make up the ground as quickly as possible. Limiting the area or space the attacker has to work with the ball. Chapter three emphasized that space equals time. Therefore, attackers should always look to pass to teammates who have space. The responsibility of the first defender is to limit the space so the attacker will not have time to pass, shoot, or dribble the ball. During game situations if a player finds himself/herself in the role of the first defender while positioned 10 to 15 yards from the attacker, he/she should:

1. Run toward the attacker quickly, possibly, before he/she has even controlled the ball.
2. Retain personal bodily control and composure.
3. Stay low maintaining a low center of gravity necessary to respond to any feints or deceptive moves initiated by the attacker.
4. Slow forward momentum within 3 to 4 yards of opponent. This will depend on the speed of an onrushing opponent.
5. When the defender is 1 to 2 yards from the opponent, place one foot in front of the other.
6. Knees bent, weight on the balls of the feet.
7. Eyes on ball.

A first defender is responsible for closing down the space between himself/herself and the attacker, moving at the ball carrier in a curved run. Don't run straight at the attacker. Cutting in front of the path that leads directly to the goal is very important. This will move the defending player immediately into the path of the goal, providing an instantaneous defense. In figure one the defending player has moved across the field first, then toward the attacker. This contrasts figure two where the defender moves directly toward ball carrier.

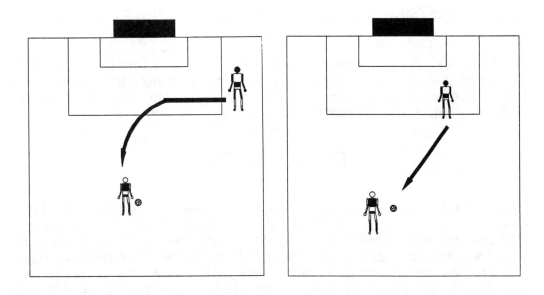

Fig. 9.1 - 9.2

If possible, the first defender should restrict the attacker from turning the ball towards his goal. The first player on defense should keep himself/herself close enough to provide appropriate pressure to where the attacker cannot turn without fear of being immediately challenged. One goal of the first player on defense is to force the attacker to play the ball back in the opposite direction. The following teaching points are used to resist an attacker from turning:

1. Keep one foot in front of the other.
2. Knees bent, weight on the balls of the feet, eyes on the ball.
3. Position oneself about 3 to 4 feet away, not too close and not too far.
4. Patiently wait for the attacker to commit.
5. Attempt a tackle when the attacker begins his turn toward your goal.

The positioning of the first defender can dictate the actions and play of the attacker with the ball. When an attacker receives a ball on the flank, the first defender has the option of channelling the opponent down the flank (disallowing him/her to play the ball in the middle) by positioning himself/herself sideways to the attacker and forcing him/her down the line. This may lead the attacking player to a teammate who can come in and support the first defender. Proper positioning can force the attacker away from dangerous areas or move him/her toward a desired direction.

Drills to Develop Skills and Techniques of the First Defender

The drill series for developing skills for the first defender is critical for all players on the field. A strong defense is created by individual players with effective defensive skills. Integrating all field players into defensive oriented drills will create a strong defensive shield.

Drill Number One

One v. One Series: This series involves four player. Players (b) and (c) are positioned in the middle of a 10 x 20 grid and players (a) and (d) are stationed at the end of each end-line of the grid. The object of the drill is to keep the attacking player from turning with the ball and completing a pass to his partner positioned at the end of the grid. At a signal, player (a) will pass the ball into player (b) who attempts to turn, and pass the ball to (d). Player (c), positioned 5 yards from (b), attempts to keep (b) from making the pass to (d). After the first attempt, player (d) passes into (c) who attempts to make a pass to (a). Player (b) is now playing the role of the first defender, and attempting to keep (c) from making a pass to (a). The drill continues in this fashion. After several passing attempts from (b) and (c), the two middle players rotate out to the end-lines and (a) and (d) rotate into the middle of the grid.

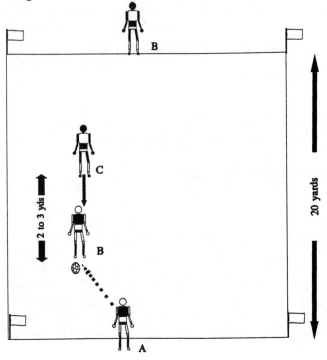

Fig. 9.3

Role of the First Defender

1.   Keep the attacker from turning.
2.   Be patient, maintain a distance between 3 to 4 feet away.
3.   Keep eyes on ball.
4.   When the attacker attempts a turn, or when he/she is half-turned, move in and make the tackle.

Drill Number Two

One v. One Series first Revision: This drill is the same as the previous drill with one revision. The middle players are separated 5 to 8 yards apart. The object of this drill is to keep the attacker from beating the first defender and passing the ball to the player positioned on the end-line. The objective of the first defender is to close down the space quickly, establishing a defensive stance, while patiently waiting for the attacker to make a move. The defender should move in and make the tackle at the appropriate time.

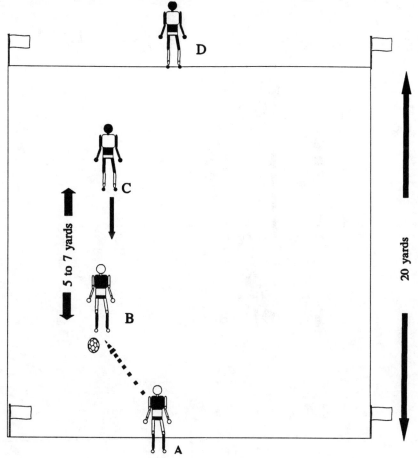

Fig. 9.4

Role of the First Defender

1. Close down the space between the defender and attacker as quickly as possible.
2. Maintain bodily control and composure.
3. Stay low, knees bent. Keep one foot in front of the other.
4. Patiently wait for the appropriate time to make the tackle.

Drill Number Three

One v. One Second Revision: This drill is the same as the previous two with the exception defending player, who is now placed 10 yards from the attacker. The object is for the first defender to close down the space, direct the running path of the attacker down one of the flanks, while initiating a tackle at the proper time.

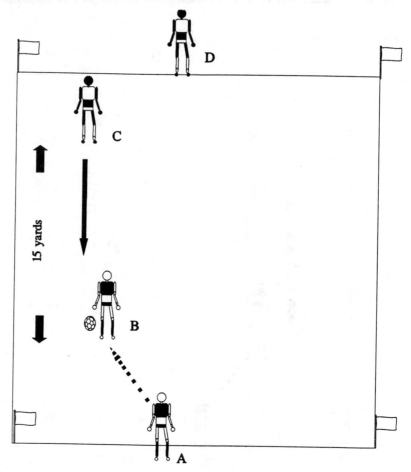

Fig. 9.5

Role of the First Defender

1. Move in quickly and maintain bodily control.
2. Once a defensive stance is established, position to where an attacker's movement can be directed.
3. When the opportunity is given make the tackle.

Role of the Instructor for each Drill

1. Reinforce the appropriate distance and positioning of the first defender.
2. Encourage players to patiently wait for the appropriate time to initiate a tackle.
3. Frequently switch the players positioned outside the grid with those inside the grid. Ensure inside players understand the strategies and skills associated with the first defender before rotating.

Performance Benefits of One v. One Drill Series

1. In a game related situation, it allows players the opportunity to perfect the skills associated with the first defender .
2. Develops many of the individual skills and techniques in a controlled environment.

Skills of the Second Defender

The second defender is responsible for supporting the first defender by playing a vital role in the protection of his/her goal. The location of the ball, or the number of attackers located in the immediate area, will reflect the positioning of the second defender. Adequate cover and support while communicating to the first defender is needed for success. Explaining what to do, where to direct the attacker, and when to tackle are the roles of the second defender. The responsibilities of the second defender include the following:

1. **Communication to the first defender**: Providing direction which gives the first defender confidence to move and tackle more freely.

2. **Cover and Support**: Cover refers to protecting a certain area. Supporting pertains to helping and backing the first defender if a tackle is inadequately executed. The second defender should situate himself/herself at a 45 degree angle approximately 5 to 10 yards away from the first attacker. The covering distance will vary depending on the situation. Close to a goal, or confronting superior numbers will require modifications.

Drills for the Second Defender

Learning distances, angles, and proper communication signals are required skills of the second defender. Instructors need to create situations that provide opportunities to build all the essential skills associated with the second defender. Three drills listed below provide instructors with a framework to build more advanced practice conditions.

Drill Number One

Two vs Two: During this drill three players are positioned in a grid area 20x30. During the drill a ball is passed to an attacker, positioned at the top of the grid. This attacker will attempt to dribble the ball down the end-line and pass it to a partner stationed at the center of the end-line. Two defenders, the first and second defender, are positioned in the middle section of the grid and to the opposite side of the attacker. They are attempting to keep the attacker from passing or dribbling to a respected target, then tackle and win the ball.

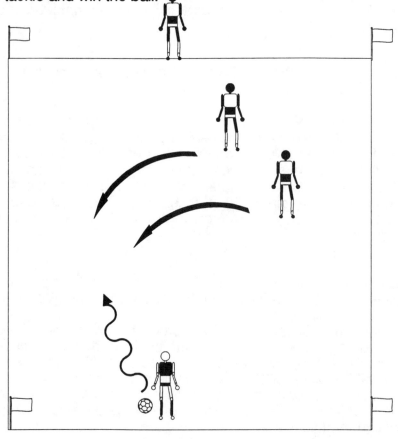

Fig. 9.6

Role of the First Defender

1. Close down the distance between defender and the attacker.
2. Move in on a curved run, getting into the path of the desired target, as opposed to a straight run at the attacker.
3. Establish proper defensive stance and positioning.
4. Patiently wait for the attacker to commit, once he loses position or control of the ball, move in for the tackle.

Role of the Second Defender

1. Close down and cover in a supporting role, establishing a position approximately 5 yards away from the first attacker.
2. Achieve a position that is 45 degrees from the first defender. Don't be caught square (parallel to first defender).
3. Provide communication, assurance, and direction to the first defender.
4. If it appears the first defender will be beaten, move in and make the tackle or be in position to become the first defender.

Drill Number Two

Two vs. Two Down the Line: The situation is the same as drill number one, except for one adjustment. Force the attacker down one side of the field. During this modification, the attacking player is now positioned at the top corner of the grid area. The two defending players are stationed in the center of the opposite side of the grid. The object is for the first defender to move in and position himself/herself to one side of the attacker, attempting to make the play of the attacking player predictable. The second defender provides support, cover, and communication to the first defender.

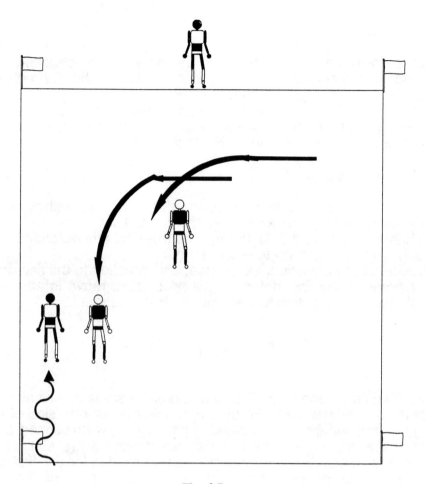

Fig. 9.7

Role of the First Defender

1. Defender needs to position himself/herself to the side, keeping knees bent, one foot in front of the other, and eyes on the ball.
2. Move and keep sideways to the attacker, forcing him/her down the side.
3. Once a corner is reached, close in and patiently wait for the right opportunity to tackle.
4. Keep the attacker from crossing. Block any attempt.

Role of the Second Defender

1. Communicate which direction the first defender needs to channel the attacking player (down the right or left flank).
2. Be firm yet controlled in your directions, precise and accurate information is needed by the second defender.
3. While angling about 45 degrees, maintain the correct distance, about 5 yards from the first defender.
4. Move in and make the tackle if the attacker gets by the first defender.

Role of the Instructor for Two vs. Two Series

1. Reinforce the correct distance and positioning of the second defender.
2. Remind the second defender to provide accurate firm communication to properly direct the actions of the first defender.
3. Demonstrate, if necessary, the proper distance, angle, and tackling technique needed to win the ball.

Performance Benefits of Two vs. Two Series

1. To create a situation that allows the second defender opportunities to analyze, practice, and execute the proper skills associated with the challenges of the position.
2. Practice skills of channeling (forcing a player to one side of the field), positioning, and tackling.
3. To reinforce the concept of patience for both the first and second defender.

The Five Principles of Defensive Tactics

Protecting the goal by reducing scoring opportunities is the main objective for any defensive team. When the ball is lost, every movement and decision made by each defender will determine if possession can be regained. Instructors need to introduce and educate each player in the five principles of defense. They include depth, balance, delay, concentration, and control & restraint.

Depth

Limiting the passing possibilities of the defense is a priority. One method is through a strategic staggering of each defensive player. The defensive player, who should never be caught square of his/her opponents, should stagger at a 45 degree angle from teammates. This is **depth** in defense. By creating depth, the pass and movement of attacking player is restricted. Notice figure one, player A (the first attacker) is positioned ahead of his/her teammates. All passing angles are closed. Options are limited. In contrast, figure two demonstrates lack of depth. Defenders are caught square, and passing lanes are open.

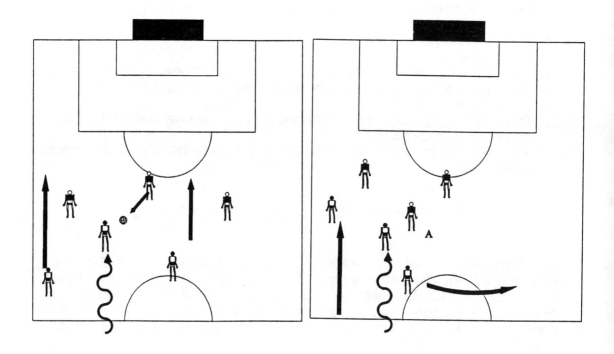

Fig. 9.8 - 9.9

Balance

The second defensive principle involves player distribution. It is termed **balance**. Balance is concerned with protection across the entire field. A team may have depth in one area, but exposed to others. The attacker will attempt to redirect his/her movements to other sections of the field. To defend these movements, a defense must control all attacking space. Marking a player making a penetrating run. Shifting a defender to an area loaded with attacking players. Providing support for front defenders. Each action helps provide balance. Contrast the two diagrams below. In figure one, two defenders are out of position. This allows attackers C and D to make penetrating runs to the middle. In figure two, balance is portrayed across the entire field. All runs are marked, and players are supporting and covering. This is balance.

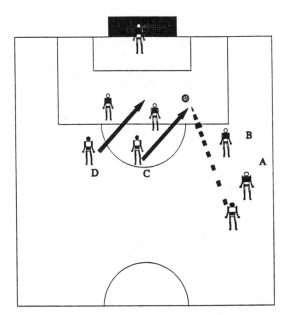 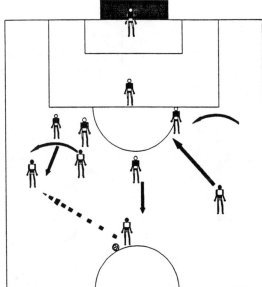

Fig. 9.10 - 9.11

Delay

Delay is the third principle of defense. This refers to the actions of players near the ball. The progress of the ball handler must be delayed so others can move in to support and cover. This is accomplished by quick man for man marking; channeling the attacker to the side-lines; or limiting passing opportunities to the middle of the field. Once the ball handlers progress is delayed, teammates can move into position. View the figure below. Attacker A leaves his/her man to delay the ball carriers progress. This allows B and C to retreat back and provide support.

Fig. 9.12

Concentration

The fourth principle is **concentration**. This element counters the offensive tactic of width. A team who maintains tight man for man defense might ultimately be separated and spread out. When a team turns to defense, the players should funnel (draw back together into the shape of a funnel) and concentrate their defense by positioning players in a tight configuration. This will limit most of the passing opportunities and increase the possibility of an interception.

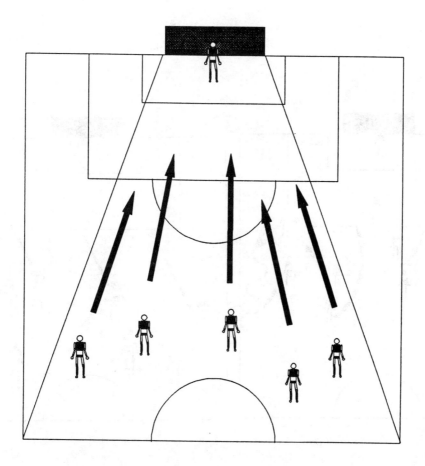

Fig. 9.13

Control and Restraint

Control and Restraint is the fifth and final principle. This concept pertains to individual encounters with opposing players. Each tackling or interception attempt must be made while maintaining bodily control. A defensive player should be confident, courageous, and determined to get that ball. Restrain from diving in too soon. Don't be overcommitted in tackling situations. Control the body, maintain balance, and move the attacker in the direction desired. This will stall the progress of an attacker, and provide time for supporting players to help. Each effort to tackle or intercept should be covered from behind. In figure one, player (A) is beaten by B. Now B will have a direct path to the goal. Before committing, ensure support and cover is provided. This will help protect the goal.

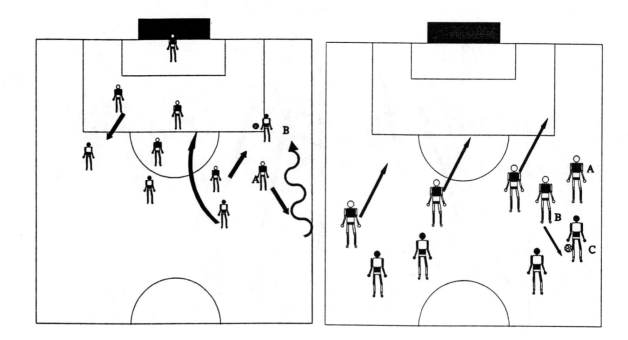

Fig. 9.14

Drills to Develop Defensive Tactics

Drill Number One

Three v. Four Drill: This drill is played on one-half of the field. Four defenders are positioned at the top of the penalty box. Three attackers move forward from the middle of the field. The object is for the defenders to steal the ball and defend their goal.

Fig. 9.15

Role of Defender

1. Support and cover each other.
2. Apply the defensive tactics of depth, balance, and delay.
3. Mark quickly, move into position with control and authority.
4. All tackles should be covered.

Role of Instructor

1. Verbalize quick and accurate movement.
2. Provide feedback on positioning and tackling.

Performance Benefits of Three v. Four Drill

1. Establishes the importance of utilizing all defensive tactics.
2. Improves on defensive skills while developing group tactics.
3. Teaches defensive positioning and movement in a game related setting.

Drill Number Two

Large Group Tactical Drill: This drill is played on a regulation soccer field with goal keepers. The field is divided into three thirds. Both ends of the field have four defenders and three attackers. The middle third has four midfielders who are separated by the mid-line. The midfield players serve as link men for the three attackers and are restricted to their third of the field. Attacking players can pass back to the midfield players at any time. Attacking players are attempting to score while the defensive players are struggling to steal the ball and play it forward. Attackers and defenders cannot cross over any restrictive line, but may pass over any line.

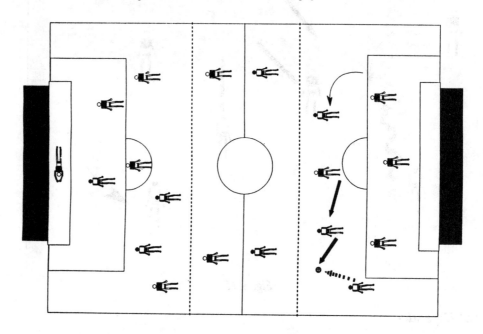

Fig. 9.16

Role of Player

1. Maintain balance and delay throughout activity.
2. Tackle with authority and cover quickly.
3. When ball is intercepted, quickly move into attack.

Role of Instructor

1. Reinforce the tactical concepts of defense.
2. Encourage one and two-touch passing.
3. Have a large number of balls ready to be replayed.
4. Verbalize the required positioning, movement, and control of all players.

Performance Benefits of Large Group Tactical Drill

1. Teaches defensive and offensive tactics.
2. Reinforces to positional roles.
3. Establishes a monitored but realistic game situation that can be stopped for instruction.

Goalkeeping

Introduction

Instructors neglect to spend time training and developing the techniques and skills of the goalkeeper. Yet, the performance of an effective goalkeeper often dictates the final result of a game. This player has a tremendous responsibility to teammates. It takes a unique person to successfully play the position of goalkeeper. This position requires strong mental and physical attributes. This chapter will introduce the instructor to basic skills and techniques associated with goalkeeping.

Stance

Proper foot placement allows for quick reaction from the goalkeeper. Bearing the weight on the toes, knees bent, and arms to the sides are desired characteristics. The goalkeeper's is encouraged to maintain this stance during each drill. When a ball handler is prepared to shoot, a goalkeeper in this stance will be ready to respond.

Teaching Points for The Goalkeeper's Stance

1. Keep head up with eyes roving the field. Follow the ball.
2. Knees are bent with weight positioned on the balls of the feet.
3. Shoulders are square. Feet separated about shoulders width apart.
4. Place arms down to the sides, with palms turned away from play. (The rationale for this method is that it is much easier to raise the hands up then bring them down.)

Photo 10.1

In this position a goalkeeper can slide back and forth on the balls of his/her feet. Movement should be in accordance to the flow of play. Scan the field, maintaining eye contact on the ball and following the movements of the players on the field.

Catching and Saving the Ball

During the game situation, goalkeeper s will face approaching balls coming from many directions traveling at various speeds. The goalkeeper needs to move in the path of the ball; determine which technique should be used to stop it; then implement the correct technique. This section will introduce six specific saving techniques applicable to various situations that occur during the game.

As indicated, a goalkeeper will confront balls at varying heights and speeds. When stopping balls above the chest, he/she should position hands with fingers pointing up. The index fingers and thumbs should be held in a "w" position (see photo 10.2). In contrast, fingers should be turned down for balls approaching below the chest. The wrists and fingers should be slightly relaxed to receive and cushion the ball during contact. Elbows should be in.

Photo 10.2

Stopping a Slow Rolling Ball

Many shots are played on the ground with limited velocity. In these situations the goalkeeper should slide into the path of the approaching ball, bend down from the waist with legs straight, point fingers toward the ground, and cup the hands to allow the ball to roll up the hands and into the arms. At this point goalkeeper will cradle the ball.

Teaching Points for Receiving a Slow Rolling Ball

1. Move into the path of the approaching ball.
2. Feet positioned a few inches apart, toes pointing toward the ball.
3. Bend down.
4. Fingers touching the ground and slightly curved.
5. Eyes on ball
6. Contact the ball into hands and allow the ball to roll up the wrist and into the arms.
7. Cradle the ball into the body pinning it to chest.

Photos 10.3 - 10.4

Common Faults and Corrections

Fault

Ball bounces off the palms and away from body.

Correction

1. Allow the ball to roll up the hands and into arms.
2. Slightly retract the hands toward the body to allow more cushion.

Fault

Ball rolls through hands and between legs.

Correction

1. Keep hands together.
2. Legs should only be separated about 1 or 2 inches.

Stopping a Fast Moving Ball or a Ball on Wet or Bumpy Surfaces

It is not uncommon for a goalkeeper to confront a fast moving ball on the ground, or a ball approaching off a wet or hard and bumpy surface. In these situations, goalkeeper's are encouraged to turn sideways to the ball, pivot on one foot, and drop down on the opposite knee. This will close any gaps between the knee and the foot. The move also creates two protective barriers to block the ball. The hands, leg and foot combination.

Teaching Points for Stopping a Fast Moving Ball on Wet or Bumpy Surfaces

1. Move across the goal into the path of the approaching ball.
2. Turn sideways toward the ball.
3. Extend the lead leg, foot turned slightly.
4. Drop opposite knee to the ground, extending the bottom portion of the leg back, parallel to goal line.
5. Keep eyes on the ball.
6. Extend arms out and receive the ball into the hands, cradle the ball into the body, pinning it against the chest.

Photo 10.5

Common Faults and Corrections

Fault

Ball travels into leg and bounces off into the field.

Correction

1. Extend arms out to receive the ball.
2. Retract the arms into the body while the ball is rolling up the forearms and into the chest.

Fault

Ball bounces off the hands and into the field.

Correction

* Allow the ball to roll up the hands and into the body. Don't use the hands as a barricade to stop the ball, but as a guide to lead the ball up and into the chest.

Stopping a Low Ball in the Air

Under the guidance of good instructors, forwards are trained to shoot low powerful shots. A goalkeeper will be required to position himself/herself in such a way to stop balls traveling low off the ground. During these situations the goalkeeper is to align himself/herself in front of the approaching ball, feet separated slightly, eyes on the ball. Just before impact, the arms are to extend out, palms facing play, with fingers extended. At the point of impact the body bends forward from the hips. Ball contacts the palms, wrists, and forearms, in that order. Then the ball is brought into the chest. To help absorb the blow, bend down and take a short hop backwards. The entire body will absorb the force of the ball while the hands cradle and pin it against the chest.

Teaching Points for Stopping Low Balls in the Air

1. Position body in line with the path of the ball.
2. Feet slightly separated, extend arms out, about 45 degrees.
3. Palms facing play, fingers extended.
4. Just before contact, bend at the waist. Keep head up, eyes on ball.
5. Slight bend at the knees.
6. Receive ball into palms, wrists, and arms, bend forward.
7. Trap ball into body with the hands.
8. Hop back to absorb the blow. Adjust movement depending on velocity of approaching ball.

Photos 10.6 - 10.7

Common Faults and Corrections

Fault

Ball bounces off hands or arms and into the field of play.

Correction

1. Retract the hands during contact.
2. Use the hands as guides to lead the ball into the arms.

Stopping a Shot Chest High

During the course of the match, a goalkeeper will also face balls approaching chest high. These conditions call for a different technique. When a ball is approaching the goalkeeper, he/she should align themselves in the pathway of the ball. Keep feet apart about shoulders width and knees bent. Extend arms out and place hands in the "W" position. Palms should face play with fingers extended. Maintain eye contact with the ball. Receive the ball into the palms Retract the arms, cushioning the ball into the chest.

Teaching Points for Stopping a Shot Chest High

1. Position body in line with the path of the ball.
2. Feet separated, knees bent, weight on balls of feet, eyes on the ball.
3. Extend arms out, palms facing play and fingers creating the "W" formation.
4. Receive the ball into the palms and retract the arms cushioning the ball into the body.

Photos 10.8

Common Faults and Corrections

Fault

The ball bounces off the chest and into the field.

Correction

1. Don't attempt to make an initial trap between the hands and the chest, allow the hands to absorb the blow first, then withdraw the hands into the chest.

Stopping balls Approaching Above the Head

It is not uncommon for a goalkeeper to confront balls above the head. Opposing players will try to cross a ball into the center on the goalkeeper's box in an attempt to shoot or head the ball on goal. The crosses (passes from the corners or sides of the field) that occur from a winger or corner-kick require a goalkeeper to practice stopping balls above his/her head. When a goalkeeper confronts this situation, he/she should jump off one foot, extending the knee up while raising both arms up with fingers extended. Create the "W" formation to receive the ball. Attempt to contact the ball at the highest possible point, keeping the ball from opponent's reach. When contact is made with the turf, secure the ball into the chest.

Teaching Points for Stopping a Ball Above the Head

1. Position body in line with the path of the ball.
2. Eyes on the ball. Judge the timing of the jump.
3. Jump off one foot, thrusting the knee up.
4. Extend the arms up, creating a "W" with the fingers.
5. Make contact with the hands.
6. Secure ball into the chest after landing on the turf.

Photos 10.9 - 10.10

Common Faults and Corrections

Fault

Ball bounces off hands and away from goalkeeper.

Correction

1. The wrists of the hands should not be stiff.
2. Absorb the blow by drawing the hands toward the body.

Fault

The timing of jump is off.

Correction

1. Observe the angle, distance, and speed of the ball.
2. Move in the direction of the ball and execute the proper jumping technique ensuring maximum height.

The Diving Save

A team scores goals by shooting low, powerful shots away from the goalkeeper. These type of shots are the most difficult to save. A goalkeeper needs to master the diving save to defend the delivery of these shots. When challenged with a ball traveling a foot or two off the ground, either to the right or left side of the goal, the goalkeeper needs to quickly respond. He/she should push off with the inside foot (the foot closest to the ball) while driving the arms up toward the head. This will help generate momentum. Contact the ball with hands while landing on the side, not the elbow. The ball should be cradled into the body by drawing the head and knees together.

Teaching Points for the Diving Save

1. Push off the inside leg.
2. Drive the arms and opposite knee up.
3. Extend arms and hands out to receive the ball.
4. Make contact with the ball and pin it to the ground with one hand behind the ball and the other on top.
5. Land on side, turning shoulder under the body.

Photos 10.11 - 10.12

Common Faults and Corrections

Fault

Ball slips through the hands and into the goal.

Correction

1. Hands and wrists should be held firm, cushion will come from the arms.
2. Keep the hands together.

Fault

Goalkeeper lands on the elbow.

Correction

* While in the air, turn the body slightly, exposing the side to the ground.

Punching the Ball Away

Often a goalkeeper cannot get close enough to the ball to catch and save it. This is often due from fast traveling balls. Another challenge occurs when opposing players will play the ball into a crowd of players near the middle of the goal box. It would be unsafe to attempt a save. When these situations arise, the goalkeeper needs to punch the ball away. Traditionally, two types of punching techniques have been taught; the two handed punch and the one hand punch.

When executing either punch, the goalkeeper should position himself/herself in line with the path of the ball. Keep the shoulders square. Jump off one leg and drive the knee of the opposite leg up. This will help to generate momentum and protect the body from approaching players. Eye the path of the ball into the fist(s). While you extend the arm(s) toward the ball, put the hand(s) into fist(s). Punch into and through the ball, to a chosen direction. The teaching points for both techniques are the same.

Teaching Points for the Punch

1. Move into the path of the ball, keeping the shoulders square.
2. Jump off one leg and drive the knee of the opposite leg up.
3. Select the direction to send the ball.
4. Extend arm(s) into the direction of the ball, make fist(s) with the hands.
5. Forcefully drive the fist(s), keeping them together, into and through the center of the ball.
6. Land on both feet, observe the location of the ball.

Photos 10.13 - 10.14
The One Handed Punch

Photos 10.15 - 10.16
The Two Handed Punch

Common Faults and Corrections

Fault

The ball does not travel in the desired direction.

Correction

1. Decide where to place the ball before punching it.
2. Align the body in the direction the punch is intended to travel.
3. Contact the ball on the flat surface of the fist(s).
4. Punch the ball toward the selected direction.

Fault

The punch lacks power and velocity.

Correction

*   Drive the fist(s) into the ball, don't tap it.

Goal Keeping Drills

The ability to handle various challenges with confidence only arrives from specialized training. The goalkeeper will confront shots traveling at various speeds, directions, and angles. Stopping a ball on a dry hard surface is different than a soft one. Goalkeeper preparation is critical. This section will include drills designed to cultivate all the techniques associated with the position. The role of the instructor and player are indicated throughout the explanation of each drill.

Drill Number One

Serving the ball to a Kneeling Goalkeeper: During this drill a goalkeeper is positioned 10 yards from a server who is distributing balls at various heights, angles, and speeds. The goalkeeper receives and controls the ball, then rolls it back to the server. After the goalkeeper improves he/she should rise to his/her feet and continue with the drill.

A   B

Fig. 10.1

Drill Number Two

Drop Kicking a ball to the Goalkeeper: During this drill, two players are positioned with balls 3 yards apart and 5 to 10 yards from the goalkeeper. Upon the signal, one participant will drop kick a ball to the goalkeeper who is attempting to save it. After each save, the goalkeeper rolls the ball back to the player while preparing to receive another shot from the second player. The players drop-kicking are attempting to place the ball at various heights while altering the speed.

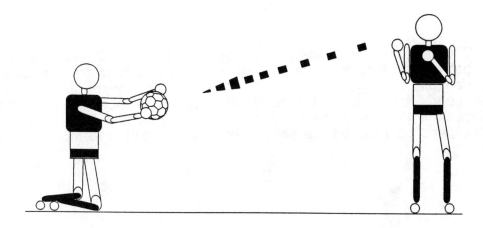

Fig. 10.2

Drill Number Three

Goalkeeper in the Middle: During this drill two shooters are positioned 8 yards apart. Each has a ball. One goalkeeper positioned between the two shooters is placed between two flags six yards apart. Outside players will take turns shooting at the goalkeeper who saves, returns, and turns 180 degrees to receive another shot from the opposite player. Shooters are encouraged to vary the heights and speeds of each shot. As the goalkeeper becomes proficient, the outside players can be moved back 15 yards with goals enlarged 8 yards.

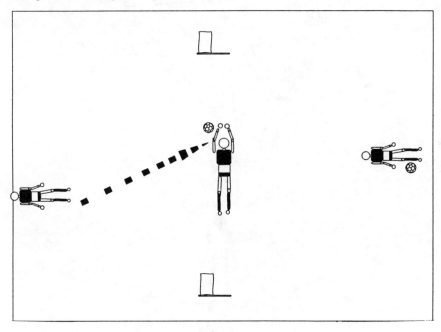

Fig. 10.3

Drill Number Four

Five Shooting on Two: During this drill five players with one ball are arranged around a circle 30 yards in diameter. Three flags are positioned in a triangular formation in the middle of the circle, 6 yards apart. Two goalkeeper's are stationed by the outside flags. The objective is for the goalkeeper's to defend the three goals created by the flags. As the goalkeeper's gain mastery, a second ball can be added to increase the challenge.

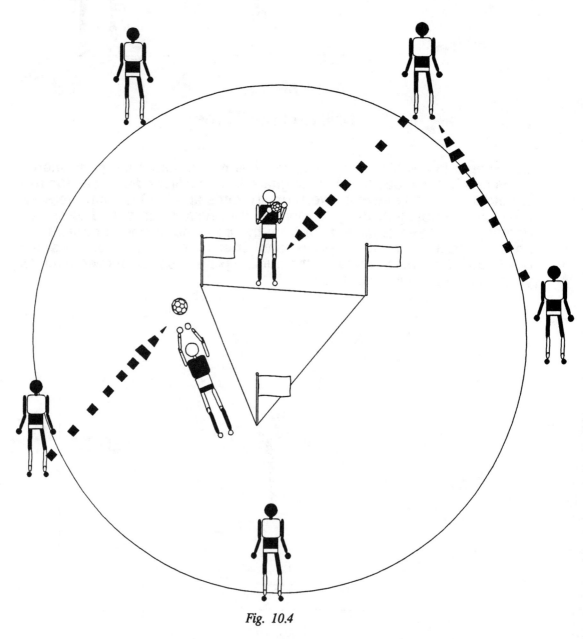

Fig. 10.4

Distributing the Ball

Proper distribution of a ball by the goalkeeper to a teammate streaking down the field can be an effective scoring opportunity. When the goalkeeper has possession, he/she is the first attacker. From this position a quick and effective counter attack can begin. Several methods of dispensing the ball exist. Each with a specified purpose. Ball distribution with the hands are designed for accuracy; while using the feet is for distance. This section will include four specific techniques: (1) rolling the ball with the hands, (2) the baseball and (3) javelin throw, and (4) punting the ball.

Rolling the Ball

Game situations require a goalkeeper to release the ball to a teammate quickly and accurately. The best method for these circumstances is rolling the ball. To effectively execute this technique, the goalkeeper will face the target while holding the ball in the palm of the hand. The arm back will be drawn back while simultaneously stepping forward with the opposite foot. The arm extends forward to roll the ball on the ground. This closely resembles a bowling ball action.

Teaching Points for Rolling the Ball

1. Face the intended target, toes pointing straight.
2. Eye the target.
3. Cup the ball into the palm of the hand.
4. Draw the ball back behind the hip.
5. Step with the opposite foot and simultaneously bring the arm forward, releasing the ball onto the ground in a bowling fashion.

Photos 10.17 - 10.18

Common Faults and Corrections

Fault

Ball does not roll to the intended target.

Correction

1. Point the toes in the direction of the target.
2. Maintain eye contact with the target.
3. Roll the ball in the direction of the target.

The Baseball Throw

Another method for distributing the ball is the baseball throw. This technique will generate more speed and distance than rolling the ball. It is effectively used when throwing the ball between defenders and to the feet of a teammate. When using this method, the goalkeeper will draw the ball back behind the ear, take a step forward with the opposite foot, while bringing the ball forward in the direction of the target. Snap the wrist at the point of release. Finish the move with a complete follow-through.

Teaching Points for the Baseball Throw

1. Face the intended target, toes pointing straight.
2. Maintain eye contact with the target.
3. Hold the ball in the palm.
4. Draw the ball back behind the ear.
5. Simultaneously step forward with the opposite foot. Bring the arm forward. Snap the wrist at the point of release.
6. Bring the arm across the body for a complete follow-through.

Photos 10.19 - 10.20

Common Faults and Corrections

Fault

Ball does not travel to the intended target.

Correction

1. Eye the target during the entire technique.
2. Toes pointed in the direction of the target.
3. Step in the direction of the target. Release the ball with a complete follow-through.

The Javelin Throw

The javelin throw is the throwing technique that will produce the greatest throwing distance. Slightly more accurate than punting the ball, the javelin throw is used by many goalkeeper's. To properly execute the javelin throw, the goalkeeper must position one foot in front of the other, cup the ball into the palm, fingers and wrist, while drawing the ball behind the hip. Bend the upper trunk over the back foot. The opposite arm will swing forward in the direction of the target for balance. When ready to release, the arm will hook forward in a half circle fashion, the hand will release the ball when it is positioned in front of the head.

Teaching Points for the Javelin Throw

1. Place one foot in front of the other with the lead foot pointing into the direction of the target.
2. Eye the target.
3. Cup the ball into the palm, fingers, and wrist.
4. Draw the ball back behind the hip; bring the opposite arm forward for balance.
5. Bend the upper trunk back over the back leg.
6. Propel the ball forward with a whip like hooking fashion. Release the ball when positioned in front of the head.
7. After release swing the arm across the body for a complete follow through. Simultaneously step forward in response to the forward motion generated by the throw.

Photos 10.21 - 10.22

Common Faults and Corrections

Fault

Ball is thrown too high.

Correction

1. Arm movement should be about a 35 degree angle.
2. Release the ball just in front of the head. Don't wait too long.

A goalkeeper will also kick the ball as a distribution method. This method will increase the distance a goalkeeper can send it, but it is less accurate. Practicing the punt will add to the arsenal of weapons used in attack. A well placed punt to "on-rushing" forwards is a tremendous threat to defenders.

Punting the Ball

When a goalkeeper decides to punt the ball he/she is looking to move the ball as far up the field as possible. This technique is very effective when a goalkeeper spots a poorly marked teammate open in the middle of the field. To properly execute this technique, the goalkeeper will first eye the desired target, then point the body in the direction of the target. Extend the arms forward while holding the ball in both hands. Take a step in the direction of the target and drop the ball in front of body. While watching the decent of the ball, bring the kicking leg up and make contact with the top of the instep. Maintain a firm ankle throughout the kick. Drive the leg into and through the ball. Land on the leg opposite the kicking foot.

Teaching Points for Punting the Ball

1. Eye the desired target and position the body in line with the object.
2. Hold the ball in both hands and keep eyes on the ball.
3. Release the ball and drive the kicking leg into and through the ball. Maintain a firm and rigid ankle.
4. Extend the leg forward and up.
5. Keep head steady.
6. Contact the ball with the top of the instep.
7. After contact, continue the upward motion to ensure proper follow through.
6. Land on the foot opposite the kicking leg. Regain balance.
7. Spot the location of the ball.

Photos 10.23 - 10.24

Common Faults and Corrections

Fault

The punt is off target.

Correction

1. Align the body in the direction of the target.
2. Make sure the follow through is straight and in line with the target.
3. Contact the ball with the top of the instep.
4. Eye target before kick.

Positioning of the Goalkeeper

A goalkeeper is continuously changing his/her position in relation to the movement of the ball. Maintaining the basic stance, and sliding side to side across the goal line, is critical. Proper positioning is also important for passes played from the corners. Encounters with ball handles who have broken free from the defense require a specific positioning.

When dealing with balls played from the corners, the goalkeeper must locate the correct position and judge the height and speed of the ball. These passes require the goalkeeper to position himself/herself 3 to 4 yards from the near post (the post closest to the ball) and 1 to 2 yards off the goal line. The near post is the greatest threat and it must be defended.

If the ball travels over the head of the goalkeeper, he/she should turn, facing the ball, and slide across the goal line to defend the opposite side.

The second positioning challenge a goalkeeper confronts is dealing with the breakaway. The goalkeeper should leave the goal line and rush out to close down the shooting angle. The goalkeeper must first determine the correct positioning in relation to the angle the attacker is approaching. As viewed in the photos below, the goalkeeper who leaves the goal line and pursues the ball carrier will limit the shooting angle. If he/she stays on the line, the entire goal area is open.

Photos 10.25 - 10.26

When the space between the goal and the ball handler is narrowed, the shooting angle is decreased. Once the angle has been determined, the goalkeeper moves toward the attacker. He/she slides parallel to the goal line (Figure 10.5), creating the largest obstacle possible to block the goal. When he/she reaches the ball carrier, he/she extends arms and legs out with palms facing the ball. This will limit most shooting possibilities.

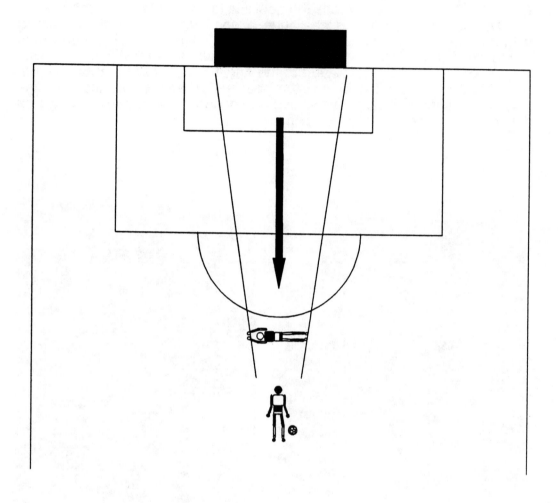

Fig. 10.5

Chapter Eleven

Systems of Play

Introduction

The organization of field players will reflect the strengths and weakness of a team. This arrangement is referred as "systems of play." Instructors will implement various systems depending on player ability, temperament, work rate (level of effort exerted), age and experience. However, no system alone can win games. As stated by Hughes (1981) "The importance of systems of play is exaggerated, and it should be understood that at the outset that there is no system which will overcome inaccurate passing or inaccurate shooting, there is no system which caters to players who will not support each other and there is no system which caters to players who will not or cannot run."
(p. 7).

When developing a system of play, instructors will arrange players in three distinct sections, back players (fullbacks), midfielders, and forwards (strikers or wingers). The roles of the players positioned in each section may vary. For example, not all midfield players will be used as link men, or support players for the fullbacks and forwards. A midfield player may be used as a defensive player to mark the striker from the opposing team. Yet, general responsibilities do exist for players positioned in the three distinct sections.

Chyzowych (1978) developed a list of fundamental responsibilities for each section of players on the field. Some of these responsibilities are a review from the five principles of attack and defense. Chyzowych's list includes introductory aims or objectives, and major positional responsibilities.

Defensive Principles

(AIMS / OBJECTIVES - Deny-Destroy-Develop)

1. Immediate Chase (pressure)
2. Fall Back and Delay (retreat, jockey)
3. Concentration (funnel), Man to Man
4. Balance (depth, or support)
5. Control / Restraint (challenge for the Ball)

Midfield Principles

(AIMS / OBJECTIVES - Build-Connect-Support)

1. <u>Slow Buildup</u>

   a. Maintain Ball Possession
   b. Dribble into Open Space
   c. Combination Passing
   d. Total Team Support
   e. Change Speed of Ball
   f. Change Direction of Ball
   g. Develop Attacking Rhythm

2. <u>Quick Counterattack</u>

   a. Rush into Open Space
   b. Use Through and Cross Passes
   c. Accelerate Support
   d. Quick Shot on Goal

Attacking Principles

(AIMS / OBJECTIVES - Move-Receive-Finish)

1. Mobility (running into open space with and without ball)
2. Combination Play (passing for depth, width, penetration)
3. Improvisation (dribbling)
4. Support (depth)
5. Finish (shooting on goal)

Various systems are designated by a numerical arrangement. These numbers represent the number of players positioned in each section of the field, and the list of numbers is sequenced from the back players to the front players. The first group of numbers applies to the back players, the second group refers to the midfielders, while the third group pertains to the forwards.

Four Contemporary Systems of Play

The 3–4–3 or WM System

The 'WM' system was the first real system developed in contemporary soccer. This system was first introduced in the early 1950's by Herbert Chapman, former manager of the famous English professional team, Arsenal. The concept behind the system was to counteract all the goals being scored by Center Forwards against his team. Manager Chapman decided to drop the center midfield player back, and make him a more defensive minded midfield player.

The 3-4-3 arrangement involves three back players, one positioned on each flank and one in the middle. It includes four midfield players, two attacking minded midfielders, and two defensive minded midfielders. The system concludes with three forwards, one on each wing and one striker positioned in the middle of the field.

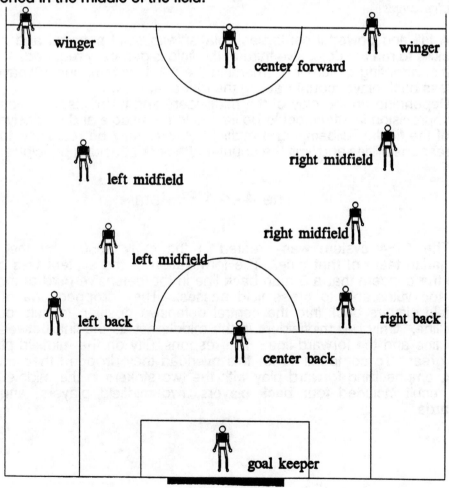

Fig. 11.1

Advantages and Disadvantages of the 3–4–3 System

Advantages

1.   Midfield section is very strong with having four players.
2.   Allows for tremendous support and depth in attack. When the ball is in the attacking third of the field, the formation allows for five attackers. .
3.   If appropriately played, it allows the two midfield players the opportunity to quickly support the defensive third of the field and create five defenders.
4.   Depending on the work rate and speed of the midfielders, the 3-4-3 system produces five attackers, four midfielders, and five back players.
5.   Improvision and cover is easily achieved, players can move from one area to the next with relative ease. If a fullback executes an overlapping run, the midfielder on that side can easily pull back and cover.

Disadvantages

1.   A tall and powerful centerback player with solid physical and mental skills to run the defensive third of the field is generally required.
2.   If confronting a team implementing the 4-2-4 system, one will have one less back player counteracting the four attackers.
3.   Depending on the play of the midfielders and fullbacks, the width and improvision in attack could be limited in the middle and defensive third of the field. Fullbacks and midfield players may be restricted to their responsibilities and limit the counter attack or attacking principles.

The 4–2–4 System

The 4-2-4 system was created in the early 1950's by the great Hungarian team of that time. The formulation of the system was based from the concern that a 3 man back line in the defensive third of the field was too vulnerable to cross field passes. They dropped one of their midfield players back into the central defensive position to help out the back line. Only two midfielders in the middle act as the link between the back line and the forward line. The responsibility on the midfield players was great. To compensate for this overload they dropped their wingers back, emphasizing forward play with the two strikers in the middle. The end result included four back players, two midfield players, and four forwards.

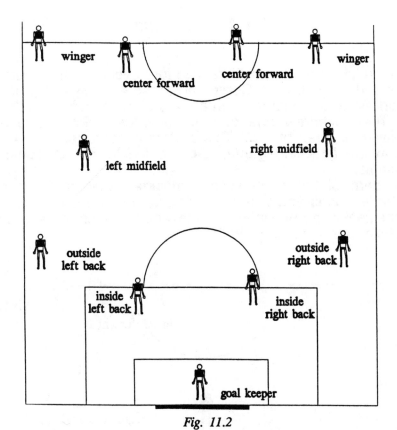

Fig. 11.2

Advantages and Disadvantages of the 4–2–4 System

Advantages

1. Allows for outside back players to move forward into the attacking position.
2. Six players can be in attack and six players can pull back in defense very quickly, with effective midfielders.
3. If properly executed, this system provides width and support in the attacking third and depth and balance in the defensive third of the field.

Disadvantages

1. Places an overwhelming burden on the two midfielders.
2. May limit the connection between the back line and the forwards.
3. May allow the opposing team to dominate play in the middle of the field; a critical section that often will dictate the flow of the game.
4. Midfielders must be tremendously disciplined and knowledgeable about their roles and responsibilities, and quickly delay the counter attack when possession is lost, or the opposing team will counter with numerical superiority.
5. Midfield players may be isolated between the four forwards and four attackers, limiting the effectiveness of the system and team.

The 4–3–3 System

The legendary Brazilians are credited for developing this system in the late 1950's and early 1960's. Compared to the 4-2-4 system, they figured that the midfield was too large of an area to cover effectively with only two players. They withdrew one of their forwards which produced three midfield players instead of two. This system encourages the fullbacks to take part in the attacking game, a characteristic of the contemporary Brazilian teams.

The pattern of the 4-3-3 system includes four back players, two covering the outsides and two in the middle, three midfield players, two covering the flanks and one in the middle, and three forwards, two wingers and one striker position in the middle.

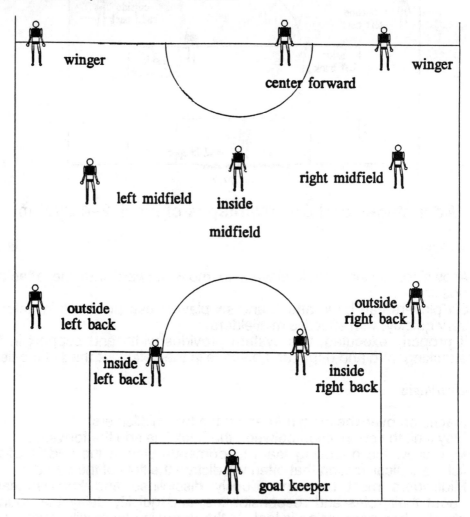

Fig. 11.3

Advantages and Disadvantages of the 4–3–3 System

Advantages

1. Provides balance across the entire field of play.
2. Connects all three sections of the field, the attacking, middle, and defensive thirds of the field. This system is effectively designed for a developmental build from the back to the front. This concept refers to ball movement. Moving the ball through all three thirds of the field with quick controlled passes.
3. Allows for tremendous support and balance in attack and defense.

Disadvantages

1. An overlapping fullback from the opposing team creates a dangerous situation in a counter attack.
2. Depending on the player's positioning and knowledge, the attack may be limited in the deep middle of the field, and the opposing defense may have numerical superiority.

The 4–4–2 System

In the 1966 World Cup final the English National Team beat Germany using the 4-4-2 system, a modification of the 4-2-4. Sir Alf Ramsey, England's National Team coach during the time, was credited for developing the system. At the time, Coach Ramsey had a definite lack of wingers, so he decided to pull the wingers back into the midfield and emphasize the attack with his two tall forwards. They would play the ball back to the onrushing midfield players for scoring opportunities. Ramsey also utilized the fullbacks in the attack by having them overlap in the place of the wingers, attempting to cross the ball into the middle of the goal keeper box.

The 4-4-2 arrangement includes four back players, two on the wings and two in the middle, four midfield players, two on the flanks and two in the middle, and two strikers.

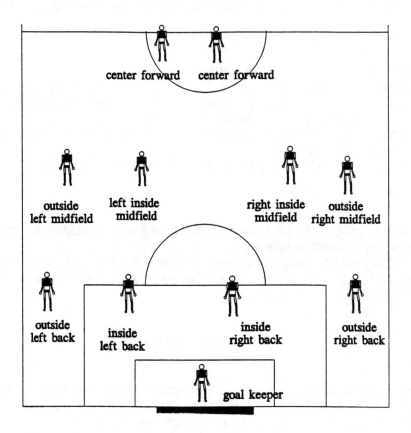

Fig. 11.4

Advantages and Disadvantages of the 4–4–2 System

Advantages

1. Creates a solid unit in the defensive third of the field.
2. Allows for a strong connection between the defensive third and the middle third.
3. If properly played, allows for improvision and creativity in attack that can unbalance an opponent.

Disadvantages

1. Limits attack and creates a low scoring game.
2. Need a certain type of player to be placed in the forward position or goals will not be scored as easily.
3. Without proper spacing, this system causes congestion and bunching of players. Certain midfield players may be lost during play, thus limiting your numbers on the field.

Instructors and players must understand that movement is the key. If players are unwilling to continuously move and search to create open space, support players, initiate passing combinations, and work together throughout the entire game, no system will help. Instructors are reminded to create a system that matches the abilities, maturity, and skill of the players representing the team. Instigating a system that looks or sounds good but doesn't match the ability of the players will generally fail. Cater the system to the players, not the players to the system.

Attacking and Defending Tactics in Restarts

Introduction

Over fifty percent of all goals scored in a game occur from restart situations (Luxbacher, 1986). Restarts or "set pieces" are situations during the game where a player has been fouled and the referee has awarded the indirect or direct free kick. Additionally, a restart will also occur if the ball has traveled out of bounds. This will result in either a corner-kick, goal-kick, or throw-in. Attacking and defending restart situations often decide the outcome of the match. It will be evident to the spectator when a coach has spent time preparing players to effectively position and arrange themselves during restart situations. With such a high percentage of goals scored in these situations, instructors are encouraged to initiate a sufficient amount of practice time teaching the tactics of attacking and defending restarts.

This chapter integrates both the attacking and defensive tactics associated with restarts. The first section will introduce indirect and direct free kicks, followed by corner-kicks and throw-ins, then conclude with penalty kicks.

Attacking Tactics in Indirect and Direct Free Kicks

Depending on the intent and severity of a foul, a player will either be awarded a indirect or direct free kick. If granted a direct free kick the offensive team has an opportunity to score directly from the spot of the foul. If the referee grants an indirect free kick, the offensive team has an opportunity to shoot on goal after the ball is first touched by any other player on the field. When awarded either a direct or indirect free kick, the attacking team should consider the following:

1. Immediately arrange players in a predetermined configuration that was set up in practice, depending on the location of the ball.

2. Attempt to deceive the defense on the intentions, purpose, and strategy of the designed play, a play that should be made simple with limited touches on the ball.

4. Attempt to block the goal keeper's vision.

5. Follow every shot by having certain players converge into the goal area in case of a rebound or if deflection occurs.

Multiple plans for attacking during a restart exist. Each option listed (Figures 12.1 - 12.3) can be modified to meet the individual talent levels of a team. Deception is the key. When a free kick is properly executed, goals are usually scored.

Optional Plans for Free Kicks

Fig. 12.1
Option One: Play Inside of Wall

Fig. 12.2
Option Two: Play Over Wall

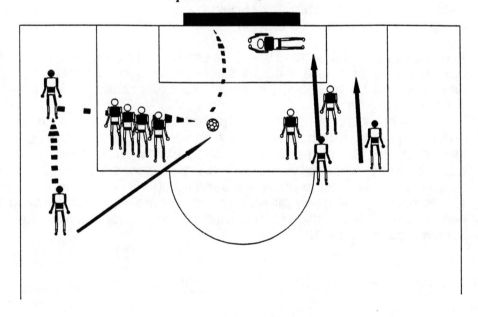

Fig. 12.3
Option Three: Play Behind Wall

Defending Tactics in Indirect and Direct Free Kicks

One of the most challenging situations to defend is indirect and direct free kicks. There is no other situation in the game of soccer where a team can force opponents 10 yards away from the ball while initiating a predetermined plan of attack. When a defensive team finds themselves defending during a free kick situation, they must do the following:

1. Arrange themselves into a wall.
2. Mark dangerously placed attackers.
3. Seal off vital space where goals are often scored.

Building the Wall

The goal keeper should not set up the wall. Successful attacking teams are coached to shoot immediately when granted a free kick. A goal keeper can be distracted who sets up the wall, and will usually be out of position. The wall should be created by a designated field player in the following steps:

1. Determine how many players should be on the wall. This is done by the goal keeper who calls out the desired number to teammates. (See Figure 12.4)
2. The designated wall setter should be positioned behind the ball on the opposite side of where the wall will be arranged. At this point one teammate will be positioned between the ball and the inside post, 10 yards from the ball.
3. Other players will line up next to the first player in the wall depending on the requested number. If four are needed, two should line up inside toward the middle of the field and one outside the first player on the wall. In figure 12.5, outside player (a) is positioned beyond the goal post. He/she is used to prevent a bending shot from scoring.
4. The remaining defensive players should secure vital space within the penalty box. They should also mark dangerously placed attacking players. (See Figure 12.6)

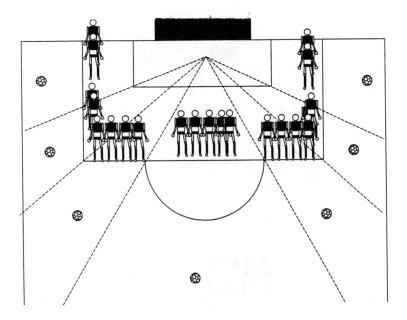

Fig. 12.4

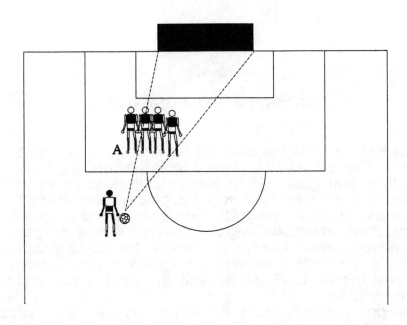

Fig. 12.5

Fig. 12.6

Attacking With Corner–Kicks

Corner-kicks provide the offensive team with another opportunity to score goals. This restart kick is granted when the opposing team kicks the ball over their own goal. When teaching attacking tactics during the corner-kick, instructors are encouraged to practice plays that will open up space near and/or around the goal. The creation of this space will depend on the deception, timing, and angle of the various runs instigated by the attacking players. When taking a corner-kick, the player should consider four distinct options with a prearranged signal and play. Options include the near post (Figure 12.7), the far post, the short corner, and the long corner (Figure 12.8).

The far-post corner is an attempt that places the ball at the center or back portion of the penalty box. The ball is usually chipped in the air to an onrushing attacker about 10 to 12 yards from goal. Often, this is challenging to the goalkeeper who must determine if he/she should leave goal-line and pursue the ball. The near-post corner is very different. This tactic utilizes a hard, low pass across the center of the goal box. If successfully executed, the ball might be deflected into the goal by an another attacker or defender.

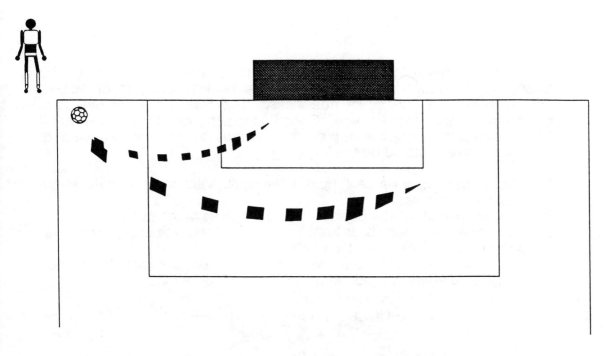

Fig. 12.7

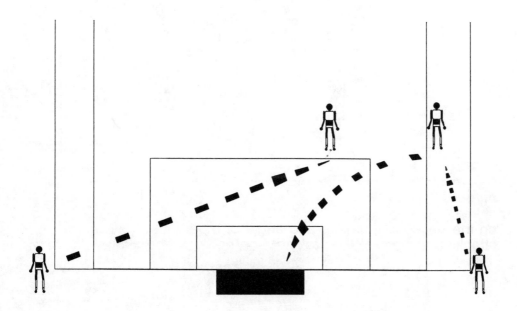

Fig. 12.8

Defending Corner–kicks

When the opposing team is awarded the corner-kick, the defensive arrangement of players is based on a similar tactical configuration as with defending indirect and direct free kicks. The first priority of defensive players is to seal off vital space. Once this is achieved, they should mark tall or dangerous opposing players. When the corner is awarded, defensive players should do the following:

1. Station one player on each post of the goal. Vital covering area where goals are often scored.
2. Goal keeper should be positioned in the middle of the goal.
3. Place one player ten yards from the ball. This will limit the short or near post options of the attacking team.
4. Have the remaining defensive players station themselves at their designated areas around the goal box (See Figure 12.9).

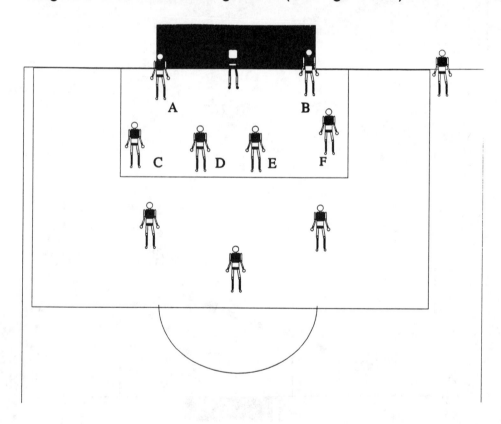

Fig. 12.9

Throw-ins

When the ball is kicked out of bounds along the side of the field a throw-in is awarded to the team who did not force it out of play. Effective teams have used this opportunity to create scoring opportunities. Successful outcomes occur when a team opens up vital space in the defense with either a dummy run or penetrating run. A common area to throw the ball is down the wings or flanks of the field. A player cannot be offside with a throw-in, so depending on the location of the ball, a team can take advantage of this situation by placing a player ahead of all others.

The long throw is becoming more and more common. This type attempts to throw the ball into the dangerous areas of the penalty box. Players who possess this ability provide teams with another scoring option. Teams are encouraged to develop plays that utilize this skill.

Defending The Throw-in

When a team is confronted with the challenge of defending a throw-in, similar principles apply as to defending any other restart situation. Players should consider the following:

1. Mark opposing players immediately, especially those near and around the ball.
2. Be aware of the dangerous space located near the goal and secure it.
3. Concentrate, then react as quickly as possible. Attempt to destroy any set play from the throw-in.

Penalty Kicks

The penalty kick is awarded to an offensive team whose teammate was directly fouled in the penalty box. The ball is placed on the penalty marker, 12 yards from goal. Every player on the field, except for the goal keeper and the designated player taking the kick, must be positioned 10 yards from the ball and outside the penalty box. Instructors are encouraged to have more than one player practice the penalty kick. If the penalty shooting player is injured, a back-up player will be selected. Too often this opportunity is missed when players are not prepared to take it. Don't over look this opportunity to train and practice the penalty kick.

When a team is awarded a penalty shot, the shooter should consider the following:

1. Decide where to place the ball before kicking it. Don't change your mind in the middle of the kick.
2. Concentrate on the ball. Don't look at the goal keeper or any other player on the field. Total concentration is required for a successful outcome.
3. Shoot the ball with confidence and control, realizing the advantage.
4. When ready, relax and move toward the ball with assurance when ready.

Laws of the Game

Introduction

The sport of soccer is governed by 17 distinct laws. These laws were established by the Federation Internationale De Football Association. Minor variations of each law might exist for youth, high school, and college teams in the United States, but traditionally, each law applies to all soccer teams across the world. Since soccer is such an international game, most rules are generally simple, specific, and easy to understand.

Chapter thirteen is based off material from "Laws of the Game - Universal Guide for Referees" is printed with the expressed written consent of the Federation Internationale De Football Association (1994).

The Field of Play

The field should be rectangular in shape, from 130 to 100 yards long and 100 to 50 yards wide. The field must be marked with a distinct line no more than 5 inches wide. The middle of the field will be marked with a halfway line. On that line in the center will be a 10 yard radius circle. The goal area will be marked with a goalie box. This rectangular box is placed on the end-line in front of the goal. Placed outside the goalie box is the penalty box. This box is the area where the goalkeeper can pick up the ball with his/her hands. The box is 18 yards long and 36 yards wide. The penalty kick mark is played in the penalty box 12 yards from the center of the goal. At the top and middle of the penalty box is an arc with a 10 yard radius. This is used for penalty kicks. When the kick is taken all players must be at least ten yards from the shooter. This arc forces each player ten yards from the mark. The goals are placed on the center of the end line. They should be 8 feet high and 8 yards across (See Figure 13.1).

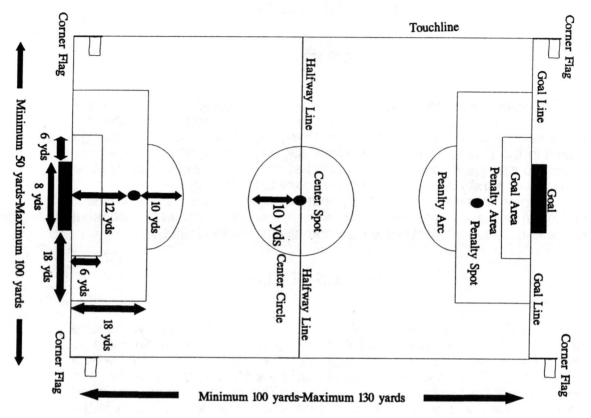

Fig. 13.1

The Ball

The size and weight of each ball will vary depending on the age classification of the player. The largest ball, size 5, is recommended for 12 years of age or older. Size 5 are between 27 and 28 inches in circumference. It should weigh between 14 and 16 ounces. (See Figure 13.2 for ball size and weight recommendations in relation to age)

Players	Ball Size	Circumference	Weight
12 and Over	# 5	27" to 28"	14 to 16oz
6 to 11	# 4	25" to 26"	11 to 13oz
Under 6	# 3	23" to 24"	8 to 10oz

Fig. 13.2

Number of Players

The game should be played by two teams with no more than 11 players per team. One player can be designated as the goalkeeper, a player who can use his/her hands within the penalty box. Again, the age of the players may vary this rule. Some leagues in American play with only 6 on the field. Check your local league for details.

Players Equipment

Uniform

The uniform must consist of shirt, shorts, stockings, shinguards, and appropriate footwear. players should not wear anything that would endanger themselves or another player.

Goalkeeper Uniform

The goalkeeper should wear colors which distinguish him/her from the other players and the referee. Padding in the elbows, hips, and knees is highly recommended. Shinguards should also be worn.

Shinguards

The shinguards must be covered by the socks. They should be made of durable material including: hard rubber, plastic, or polyurethane. This piece of equipment is very important, and should be worn by each player.

Referee

The referee is the official of the game. His/her authority commences as soon as he/she enters the field. His/her authority is maintained throughout the game, and any decision made is final. The referee is responsible for enforcing the laws of the game. Decisions he/she is accountable for include:

1. **Advantage Rule:** Used to refrain from penalizing in situations where it would be an advantage to the offending player. The referee will allow the player to continue even though he/she acknowledges an infraction occurred.

2. **Record of Game:** He/she is the official time and score keeper. The referee will also keep track of any player who receives a yellow or red card.

3. **Stopping the Game:** The referee may stop, suspend, and terminate play at any time. This may result from any infringement, injury, interference by spectators, or any situation he/she deems necessary.

4. **Yellowcard:** This card serves as a warning. When any player demonstrates misconduct or ungentlemanly behavior, the referee will show him/her the card.

5. **Redcard:** When the redcard is shown to a player, he/she is out of the game. It is given (in the opinion of the referee) when a player: (1) is guilty of violent conduct, (2) commits a serious foul, (3) uses foul or abusive language, or (4) persists in misconduct after having received a caution (yellowcard).

Linesperson

Generally two people will be linespersons. One will work the right side of the field while the other works the left side. This person has several responsibilities. He/she will signal when the ball is out-of-bounds; when a team is entitled to a corner-kick, goal-kick, or throw-in, and assist the referee in controlling the game.

Photo 13.1

Duration of the Game

The duration of the game will reflect the age of the players. Some games are played with 15 quarters while others are played with 30 to 40 minute halves. For players over 12, the duration of the game will equal two 45 minute halves. This may be altered for the following reasons:

1. allowances made due to time loss through substitution.
2. transporting injured players.
3. time wasting (discretion of referee)
4. a half-time that should not exceed 5 minutes except by consent of the referee.

The Start of the Game

The game will start with the sound of the referees whistle. Choice ends and kick-off will be determined by a coin flip. The team who wins the toss will choose either ball or end. Upon the referees signal, a player will kick a stationary ball forward. The ball must be played forward before another player can touch it. Opposing players must be 10 yards from the ball until the ball is kicked into play. After a goal is scored the game will be restarted in the same manner by a player of the team losing the goal. After half-time, players will change ends. The kick-off is taken by a player on the team that did not start the game.

Photo 13.2

Ball In and Out of Play

The ball is out of play when it has completely crossed the goal line or side line. It doesn't matter if it was in the air or on the ground. The ball is also out of play when the referee blows his/her whistle.

The ball is in play if it rebounds from a goal-post, cross-bar, or corner-flag and returns to the field of play. It remains in play if it rebounds off the referee or linesperson who is on the playing field. The ball will remain in play until the referee signals that a foul or infringement of the laws has occurred.

Method of Scoring

A goal is scored when the whole of the ball has been kicked past over the goal line and between the cross-bar and goal-posts. This is providing it has not been thrown, carried, or intentionally propelled by the hand or arm.

Off-Sides

A player is off-sides if he/she is nearer to his opponents' goal line than the ball, unless:

1. he/she is in his/her own half of the field.
2. he/she is not nearer to his/her opponents' goal line than at least two of his/her opponents. This includes the goalkeeper.

A player is declared offsides in the opinion of the referee. This can occur:

1. at the moment the ball touches or is played by one of his/her team.
2. when he/she is interfering with play or with an opponent.
3. a player is seeking to gain an advantage by being in that position.

A player shall not be called off-sides by the referee merely because he/she is in an off-side position. In addition, a player should not be called off-sides if he/she receives a ball directly from a goal-kick, corner-kick, or throw-in. When a player is declared off-sides, an indirect free kick is awarded. This kick is taken at the spot of the foul by a player on the opposing team.

Fouls and Misconduct

Two distinct kicks are awarded when a foul occurs, the indirect and direct free kick. The type of kick will depend on the severity of the foul. As previously stated, indirect free kicks must touch another player before going into the goal. In contrast, a player can score directly from a direct free kick.

1. **Direct Free Kicks** are awarded to a player when another player on the opposing team intentionally commits any of the following nine rules;

    a. Kicks or attempts to kick an opponent.
    b. Trips an opponent.
    c. Jumps at an opponent.
    d. Charges an opponent from behind unless the opponent is penalized for obstruction.
    e. Strikes or attempts to strike an opponent or spits at him/her.
    f. Holds an opponent.
    g. Pushes an opponent.
    h. Carries, strikes, or propels the ball with the hand or arm.
       (Does not apply to the goalkeeper in the penalty box.)

When a direct kick is awarded, the kick shall be taken at the spot of the foul, unless the offense was committed by a player in his/her own penalty area. When this occurs a penalty-kick is awarded.

Photo 13.3

2. Indirect Free Kicks are awarded to a player when another player on the opposing team commits any of the five listed offences.

    a. Playing in a manner considered by the referee as dangerous.
    b. Charging with the shoulder when the ball is not within playing distance, and the player is definitely not trying to play it.
    c. Intentionally obstructing an opponent, using the body as an obstacle when not playing the ball.
    d. Charging the goalkeeper except when he/she is:
        1. obstructing an opponent
        2. has past outside his/her goal area

Indirect free kicks are also awarded when the goalkeeper makes an infraction. This may be called if the goalkeeper commits any of the following violations:

    a. takes four steps with the ball after gaining control.
    b. bounces or throws the ball into the air and catches it again, without releasing it into play.
    c. Touches the ball with the hands after it has been deliberately kicked to him/her by a teammate.
    d. Indulges in tactics (under the opinion of the referee) that are designed to waste time, giving an unfair advantage to his/her own team.

When the indirect or direct kick is awarded, the kick shall be taken by the opposing side at the spot where the infraction occurred. As previously indicated, a goal cannot be scored from the indirect kick unless the ball has been played or touched by another player. The direct free kick can be scored without a second player touching the ball.

Five stipulations exist when taking either kick. They include the following:

1. All opposing players shall be at least 10 yards from the ball and shall remain 10 yards until the ball is touched.
2. The ball cannot go back to the goalkeeper. In order for it to be replayed to him/her, it must go into the field of play first.
3. The ball must be stationary before it is kicked.
4. Any free kick awarded to the defending team in their own goal area can be taken from any part within the goal-area.
5. Any indirect free kick awarded to the attacking team within its opponent's goal-area shall be taken from the part of the goal line which runs parallel to the goal line, at the point nearest to where the offence was committed.

Penalty–Kick

A penalty-kick will be taken from the penalty mark. Once the referee has placed the ball, all players shall be at least 10 yards from the ball. This rule does not apply to the one kicking the ball and the goalkeeper. When the kick is awarded, certain rules exist for both the goalkeeper and shooter. The goalkeeper must stand on his/her own goal-line, positioned between the two goal-posts, without moving the feet. He/she cannot move until the ball is kicked. The player taking the kick must strike the ball forward. He/she cannot touch it twice, unless another player has touched it.

Throw–in

When the whole of the ball passes over a touch-line (side line), either on the ground or in the air, it should be thrown in from the spot where it went out. A player from the opposite team who touched it last should throw the ball. When throwing the ball, he/she must:

1. Face the field of play
2. A section of both feet must be in contact of the ground, either on the touch-line or behind it.
3. The thrower shall have both hands on the ball and deliver it from behind the head.
4. The thrower cannot touch the ball a second time until another player has touched it.
5. A goal cannot be scored directly from a throw-in unless touched by another player before entering the goal.

Goal–kick

The goal-kick is awarded when the whole of the ball passes over the goal-line either in the air or on the ground, excluding that portion between the two goal-posts. The ball must have been last touched by an attacker. Prior to kicking the goal-kick, the ball must be placed within the goal-area. Critical points to remember about the goal-kick include:

1. The goalkeeper cannot receive the kick into his/her hands from the goal-kick.
2. If the ball is not kicked beyond the penalty-area, the kick shall be retaken.
3. The one kicking cannot play the ball a second time until a second player has touched it.
4. A goal cannot be scored directly from a goal-kick.
5. Opposing players must remain outside the penalty box until the ball has been kicked outside the penalty area.

Corner Kick

The corner-kick is awarded When the whole of the ball, either in the air or on the ground, passes over the goal line after being touched by a defending player, excluding the portion between the goal posts. When this occurs, a member from the attacking team wins the ball. This kick will take place at either corner of the field. It depends on which side the ball went out-of-bounds. When taking the corner kick, remember the following:

1. The whole of the ball must be placed and kicked within the quarter circle at the nearest corner flag or post.
2. A goal may be scored directly from the corner kick.
3. Players of the opposing team must be at least 10 yards from the ball prior to the kick.
4. The player taking the corner kick cannot touch it a second time until another player has touched it.

Photo 13.4

Glossary Of Soccer Terms

Aerobic–Exercise performed with oxygen.

Anaerobic–Exercise performed at an intensity level so high the demand for oxygen exceeds the ability to supply it.

Advantage rule–A law that allows the referee to continue play after an infraction when awarding the penalty would be a disadvantage to the team offended.

Attacker–A player on a team who has ball possession.

Ball control–Using various techniques to bring the ball under control.

Blindside run–A run by an attacker on the side of the ball opposite the defender.

Block tackle–A frontal tackle executed in an attempt to win the ball from the ball carrier.

Centering–Passing the ball from one side of the field into the center, near the goal.

Closing down–Advancing toward opponent to restrict the space between opponents.

Concentration in defense–Defensive tactic used to limit the space within the penalty box.

Cover–maintaining a close distance to an opponent, in position to challenge if one receives the ball.

Cross–See centering.

Dangerous play–Playing in a manner which could cause injury.

Defender–A player on a team without possession of the ball.

Depth–positioning that sustains proper support for attackers or defenders.

Diagonal run–A run made diagonally across the field.

Direct kick–A free kick that can be scored without touching another player.

Disguise run–An attempt to unbalance and trick the defensive player and place one out of position.

Dummy run–See disguise run.

Feinting–Action used to trick or confuse an opponent.

Flanks–Areas of the field near the side-line, approximately 15 yards.

Forwards–Players positioned in the front with predominantly offensive tasks; usually identified as wingers or strikers.

Free kick–A kick awarded to a team after an infraction. See Indirect and Direct free kick.

Fullbacks–Players positioned in the back with predominantly defensive tasks; identified as backplayers, stoppers, or sweepers.

Goal kick–A kick taken within the goal area by a member of the defending team. This team is awarded the kick after an attacking/opposing player kicks/touches the ball over the goal-line.

Goal side of the ball–A player maintains a position between the goal and an opponent.

Heading–A method of propelling the ball with the forehead.

Indirect free kick–A free kick that cannot be scored directly; the ball must first touch another player other then the kicker.

Instep–Upper surface of the foot.

Jockeying–Delaying the movement of a ball carrier, attempting to force an attacker down the flank.

Juggling–Keeping the ball in the air using various body parts except the arms or hands.

Marking–To cover an opponent closely in order to keep one from receiving the ball.

Midfielder–Players positioned between the forwards and backs. They serve as link men/women who build an attack and help the fullbacks in defense.

Mobility–Movement with and without the ball to support and create space for teammates.

Nonkicking foot–Foot used to balance the body while kicking the ball.

Obstruction–Preventing an opponent from reaching a ball not within playing distance.

One-touch passing–Passing between teammates with an instantaneous pass.

Open space–Area of the field not being covered by the opponents.

Overlap–A run made by a supporting player who moves from a position behind a teammate to a position ahead of that teammate.

Penetration–Attacking tactic used to move through the opposition's defense.

Play on–See advantage rule.

Pitch–Field of play.

Running off the ball–Individual tactical run used to support ball carrier.

Restart–A method of restarting play after the action has stopped. This includes corner-kicks, goal-kicks, indirect and direct free kicks, and throw-ins.

Set piece–Predetermined tactical move used in attack.

Shielding–Maintaining ball possession while keeping one's body between the ball and opponent.

Sliding tackle–A method of taking the ball from an opponent by sliding on one's leg and kicking the ball away.

Square pass–Pass made parallel to goal-line.

Stopper–Central defender who usually marks the center forward.

Striker–Attacking player positioned in the front of the attack; generally the primary goal scorer.

Support–A position that provides teammates either passing options or defensive cover.

Sweeper–Last defender, except goalkeeper, that plays behind the team.

System of play–Organization arrangement of all field players.

Tackle–An attempt the win the ball.

Thirds of the field–Areas symbolizing the attacking, middle, and defensive thirds of the field.

Wall pass–A passing combination that consists of two passes. One pass to a teammate who acts as a wall to deflect the ball forward for the second pass.

Width in attack–Attacking tactic to pull defenders away from central areas of the goal.

Zone defense–A defensive tactic in which defenders cover certain sections of the field.

Reference List

Benedek, E., & Palfai, J. (1978). <u>600 Games for Soccer Training</u>.
Budapest, Hungary: Corvina

Chyzowych, W. (1978). <u>The Official Soccer Book of The
United States Soccer Federation</u>. Chicago, IL: Rand McNally
& Company

Ditchfield, M., & Bahr, W. (1988). <u>Coaching Soccer the
Progressive Way</u>. Englewood Cliffs, NJ: Prentice Hall.

FIFA. (1993). <u>Laws of the Game - Universal Guide for
Referees</u>. Zurich, Switzerland: Federation INternatinoale De
Football Association.

Giles, H. (1905). <u>Adversaria Sincia</u>. In N.E. Gardner, <u>Athletics
in the Ancient World</u>. (pp. 16). The Clarendon Press.

Hughes, C. (1981). <u>Soccer Tactics and Teamwork</u>. Yorkshire,
England: EP Publishing Limited.

Luxbacher, J. (1986). <u>Soccer: Winning Techniques</u>. Dubuque, IA:
Eddie Bowers Publishing Comp.

Rosenthal, G. (1981). <u>Everybody's Soccer Book</u>. New York, NY:
Charles Schribner's Sons.

Sour, P., & Tyler, M. (1978). <u>Soccer the World Game</u>. New York,
NY: St. Martins Press.

Van Dalen, D., & Sasajima, K. (1965). Football games in
antiquity. <u>Quest</u>, <u>4</u>, 69-77.

Van Dalen, D., & Bennett, B. (1971). <u>A World History of Physical
Education</u>. Englewood Cliffs, NJ: Prentice Hall

Wade, A. (1981). <u>Coach Yourself Back Defenders</u>. Yorkshire,
England: EP Publishing Company.